ROUND ABOUT THE BALLET

*"If the leaves of a tree did not move,
how sad would be the tree–and so should we!"*
–Degas

Featuring dancers from American Ballet Theatre and New York City Ballet

ROUND ABOUT THE BALLET

William Cubberley and Joseph Carman
Photographs by Roy Round

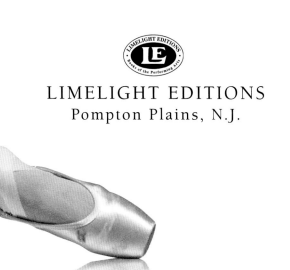

LIMELIGHT EDITIONS
Pompton Plains, N.J.

Published in 2004 by

Limelight Editions
512 Newark Pompton Turnpike
Pompton Plains, New Jersey 07444
U.S.A.

For sales, please contact

Limelight Editions
c/o Hal Leonard Corp.
7777 West Bluemound Road
Milwaukee, Wisconsin 53213 U.S.A.
Tel. 800-637-2852
Fax 414-774-3259

Website: www.limelighteditions.com

Book design by Bob Antler, Antler Designworks
Printed in China

Library of Congress Cataloging-in-Publication Data

Cubberley, William.
    Round about the ballet / William Cubberley, Joseph Carman, and Roy
Round.– 1st Limelight ed.
        p. cm.
    Includes index.
    ISBN 0-87910-311-6 (hardcover)
    1. Ballet dancers–Biography–Interviews. 2. American Ballet Theater. 3.
New York City Ballet. I. Carman, Joseph. II. Round, Roy. III. Title.
GV1785.A1C83 2004
792.8'092'2–dc22

                                                2004017682

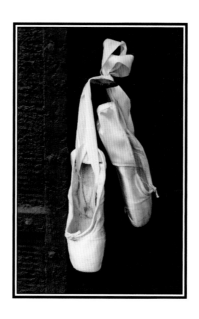

To our muse, Georgina Parkinson

CONTENTS

FOREWORD

As a child, I loved poring over the ballet photographs of Baron Nahum, professionally known simply as "Baron." Looking through Roy Round's photographs of the latest generation of stars from American Ballet Theatre and the New York City Ballet, the memory returned of those absorbing hours, for *Round About the Ballet* is a book that calls out to the avid child at the heart of most balletomanes.

Baron suggested the world through which the dancers moved, most obviously a world of glamorous dark shadows and thick makeup, of romantic characters that were as fragile as the costumes were lavish and the sets solid. Still, there was a sense that these larger-than-life ballet icons were a part of something even more momentous: the *working* world of dance. Round, whose work was predominantly fashion and advertising, started taking ballet photographs in the early sixties, thereby adding a new dimension to his already broad range of work. He entered the ballet scene just a few years after Baron's heyday in dance publishing. Round is also good at drawing the viewer into a world that is tantalizing, but somehow is not exotic.

In part, Round's photographs succeed because of their simplicity. Baron worked with shadow and light, and his studio gave little impression of depth. Round works with light and air and infinite-seeming space. True, his subjects sometimes wear costumes that place them in recognizable roles. The portraits reveal individual characteristics. The tilt of Angel Corella's head conveys, for example, the joyous central impulse of his dancing. The angle of Nikolai Hübbe's upper torso breathes nobility. Ethan Stiefel's unexpectedly haunted eyes suggest the inherent drama that lies beneath his soaring technique. But these are straightforward photographs. Round has managed to pry Stiefel loose from his ever-present motorcycle. No dancers peer through grids. No mirror images gaze back at the reader. Instead, we turn the pages to find representations of the ideal that has governed ballet from the late twentieth century on. Look at Julie Kent in arabesque here, or at Vladmir Malakhov's brises voles. Pure form is captured in these long, lean, tapering body lines.

But taken together, the photographs and accompanying essays and vivid interviews also provide a look at a different universe from the one depicted in Baron's photographs just a half-century ago. Round's subjects come from many different countries and parts of the United States, many of them refined in the gaudy firecracker-flare of the international ballet competition, an unknown ritual in those other times. Ballet has become international, though the old international star system is gone. A certain homogeneity has set in. The national styles that were barely recognized in the 1950s are known and understood today, and their characteristics have blurred. Hübbe does not have to explain who Bournonville was, for instance, but on the other hand he now seldom dances that Danish choreographer's work. Nor could he be described as a Balanchine dancer or fit into any other easily recognizable category.

Hübbe's talk about dramatic and plotless ballet, and the performing of each, is a perceptive, sophisticated analysis that has much to reveal about individual artistry in an age when ballet has become a *profession* rather than the vocation it once was of necessity. Many of Round's dancers talk of being underpaid, an interview topic that might have astonished Baron's ballerinas. They talk of receiving college degrees and what they dream about at night, of riding motorcycles and bringing Coca-Cola—not champagne!—to a desert island. They have impish senses of humor and a fondness for everyday colloquialisms. And who, in the good-old/bad-old days of Baron, could imagine a Fonteyn or Lifar answering a question with "Gosh, I don't know," as the formidable young artist Gilliam Murphy so charmingly does here, or cheerfully talking of weaknesses as a dancer when asked about strengths?

And yet Round and his collaborators have captured one of the paradoxes of ballet as we know it just after the turn of the twenty-first century. Somehow, the best dancers of this hypertechnical era have managed to retain the old joy of moving, captured so exhilaratingly here in the image of Murphy leaping, hair flying, as if for *pleasure*. And we know, after spending this time with them, that most of Round's dancers exhibit a poignant sense of indebtedness for a life that is hard, but perhaps in the end, a calling. What would she choose to ask Balanchine, Wendy Whelan is asked, if he were alive today? She would ask, this exotic veteran ballerina responds, about what she *still* needs to find in his choreography.

—Jennifer Dunning
June 2004

PREFACE

I have been fortunate enough to have photographed most of the great dancers of the last forty years—from Alicia Alonso to Svetlana Zakharova. Therefore it gives me great satisfaction to add to this roster some of the more recent dancers performing in New York City.

This book celebrates the richness of dance as seen contemporaneously in New York. All the dancers are preeminent in their field, and although not all are homegrown—some are from the United Kingdom, some from Denmark, France, Spain, South America—they nevertheless chose to show prowess and test their mettle with the most sophisticated and astute audience in the world—that of New York City. As the song tells us: If you can make it there, you'll make it anywhere.

The photographer Roy Round with Julie Kent, principal dancer of American Ballet Theatre, outside the Metropolitan Opera House in New York City

They are all stars, though most would eschew that title since they are self-effacing, conscientious workers who go to class every day, take corrections, shrug off aches and pains, go onto the stage, and make magic. I admire them enormously and thank them sincerely for giving up their valuable free time to come to my studio and work so hard to do my bidding.

Some special thanks are due to various people, including my wife, Georgina Parkinson, who helped assiduously and often brought to bear her coaching eye during the photographic sessions. Also special thanks to our son, Tobias, who did so much work behind the scenes, often using his considerable negotiating and diplomatic skills. Thank you, Tobias. My sincere thanks also to Bill Cubberley, who conceived this book and kept the project afloat. Many thanks also to Siobhan Burns of New York City Ballet for her invaluable endeavors. Last but not least, my thanks to Dick Gallen, my fairy godfather!

I dedicate my part of the book to my grandson, Thomas.

—Roy Round

Over the years, I have known many ballet dancers, and I have always admired their skill, dedication, and artistry. Anyone who has ever seen a live performance of ballet knows the thrill of seeing larger-than-life figures onstage. It is easy to wonder what these dancers are like beyond the footlights—how they acquired such amazing artistry and technique, what the joys and difficulties are in sustaining their careers, what dreams they would like to fulfill as performers. This book is an attempt to answer some of these questions for some of the leading ballet dancers working today.

Each chapter is devoted to an individual dancer, and includes a biography that charts the story of his or her career, an interview with the dancer, and studio photographs by Roy Round. Taken together, these three elements provide a unique insight into the lives of the fifteen dancers profiled.

The book is meant to be of value to both the balletomane and the uninitiated. Hopefully, those who already love the ballet will have their appreciation intensified, and those who are unfamiliar with this art form will begin seeking out its many delights. All the dancers featured in the book dance with either American Ballet Theatre or New York City Ballet. The premise of the book is easy to convey: Ballet dancers are beautiful to look at and have fascinating stories.

Collaborating with Roy Round, one of the world's leading dance photographers, and Joseph Carman, a former ballet dancer who writes extensively about dance, has been one of the many pleasures I have had in putting this book together. I am indebted to their tireless dedication to what at times seemed an impossible task.

—William Cubberley

Dancers represent an undervalued sector of society. Perhaps that is because dance, as an art form, is sometimes regarded as a poor stepsister to other art forms—music, literature, painting, and theater, for example. Nothing could be further from the truth. Movement as ritualized art predates the most primal of human expressions, perhaps even codified verbal communication. Classical ballet, at its finest, raises dance up to its most glorious, idealized form, where physical line intersects with musicality and meets the sheer brilliance of technique and drama.

Having been a dancer, I know that dancers have plenty to say, not only with their bodies, but also through the stories of their lives. Training to be a classical dancer demands an enormously concentrated period of a person's life; discipline and experience combine to mold a performer through a process that rivals alchemy. The career is all too short, but wonderfully rich and fulfilling, and any dancer who made it into these pages would not have been happy pursuing anything else in his or her young life.

These particular fifteen dancers, representative of the greatest in ballet today, have all made a home with one of New York's two great ballet companies: American Ballet Theatre and New York City Ballet. They give physical life to the choreography of masters like Balanchine, Ashton, Petipa, Bournonville, Tudor, MacMillan, and Robbins. Initiating their training in disparate places, from Brazil to Copenhagen, and from Kentucky to Kiev, they all made it to the dance capital of the world and subsequently to the top of their profession. In the field of ballet, they are the equivalents of Alex Rodriguez, Yo-Yo Ma, or Madeleine Albright in their respective professions. This book pays tribute to them through their own words and through the splendid photographs of Roy Round.

–Joseph Carman

ACKNOWLEDGMENTS

William Cubberley and Joseph Carman would like to thank the following people and organizations for their invaluable help with this book: Siobhan Burns and New York City Ballet press department, American Ballet Theatre press department, Richard Gallen, Richard Dannay, Jennifer Dunning, Tobias Round, Paul Matsumoto, James Gaskin, Alfred Szymanski, Judith Hoffman, Andrea Kelly, Todd Warner, Audrey Ross, Edward Leida, Dick Caples, Robert Hill, Peter Diggins, the Library of Performing Arts at Lincoln Center, Georgina Parkinson, Michael Avedon, New York City Ballet wardrobe department, American Ballet Theatre wardrobe department, Kevin McKenzie, Peter Martins, the Balanchine Trust, the *New York Times*, the *New York Observer, Dance Magazine*, and *Pointe* magazine.

ROUND ABOUT THE BALLET

MAXIM BELOSERKOVSKY

AMERICAN BALLET THEATRE

Russian iconography could hardly uphold a better model for a young prince than Maxim Beloserkovsky. His image might easily adorn the cover of a lacquered enamel Russian jewel box, depicting a scene of the Prince brandishing the Firebird's feather, or awakening Princess Aurora from her century of slumber with a kiss. Plenty of male dancers assume princely roles, but only a chosen few, like Beloserkovsky, are born with the regal bearing and the handsome looks to pull it off with ease.

Beloserkovsky was born in Kiev, Ukraine, a city steeped in cultural history and with a world-class ballet school. Because of his outstanding physical capability, at age five he entered the School of Dance in Kiev, the state institution that traditionally only accepted students at age seven or older. From the beginning, he was earmarked for his ideal classical appearance and style and groomed to be an Albrecht or Siegfried.

After graduation, Beloserkovsky was a principal dancer for the National Opera of Bulgaria from 1990 to 1991. He then returned home to dance with the National Opera of the Ukraine as a soloist, and in 1992 the company awarded him the title etoile. As a star in the Ukraine, Beloserkovsky excelled in the classical roles. His gracious and elegant manner, combined with perfectly shaped legs and feet, made him a matinee idol as the Prince

in *Cinderella*, Albrecht in *Giselle*, and Prince Desire in *The Sleeping Beauty*. Beloserkovsky also infused roles like Farhad in *The Legend of Love* and the pas de deux from *Le Corsaire* with his innate romantic temperament and passionate ardor.

Longing to realize his full artistic potential in the West, Beloserkovsky joined the Hamburg Ballet for a season. Although exposure to the company's contemporary choreography was valuable, he needed another environment in which to flourish. In 1994, Kevin McKenzie, the director of American Ballet Theatre (ABT), spotted him in class in New York City and offered him a corps de ballet contract on the spot, which the dancer gladly accepted. The same year, Beloserkovsky married ballerina Irina Dvorovenko, whom he had known since childhood.

In May 1995 Beloserkovsky advanced to soloist. ABT seemed tailor-made for him with its measured balance of classical and contemporary roles, and his hard work with the company immediately paid off. Among his first classical roles were Franz in *Coppélia*, Conrad in *Le Corsaire*, and Basilio in *Don Quixote*. He was aptly suited to portray Her Lover in Antony Tudor's modern classic *Jardin aux Lilas*, and Arthur Saint-Leon in Robert Joffrey's romantic period piece *Pas des Deesses*.

In August of 2000 he was promoted to the rank of principal dancer. Beloserkovsky has shone in contemporary ballets like Martha Graham's *Diversion of Angels*, Jiri Kylian's *Sinfonietta*, Robert Hill's athletic *Baroque Game*, and Twyla Tharp's spiky *Known by Heart*. Perhaps his grandest performances, ignited by the partnership with his wife, are in the classic love stories of ballet, *Swan Lake* and *Giselle*.

Did your family encourage you to dance?

My mother had an obsession with—not even the classical ballet—with the dance itself. She would watch the old movies—the Hollywood movies with Fred Astaire and Ginger Rogers—and she just cried because of the grace, the way the women looked, the men in tuxedoes, and just the *dance*. She was totally transformed. And she didn't know the classical ballet or folk dance or modern or jazz. Just any form of dance that I pursued made her happy. She was so proud! "Oh, I'm going to see *you*, my *son*, on the stage at the *Metropolitan Opera!*"

Maxim Beloserkovsky 5

Can you describe the training that you had in the Ukraine?

It was unbelievable. What we had in the former Soviet Union was an exclusive school for talented kids where you spent eight years. I didn't have a childhood at all. I didn't have time to play or just to have sort of a normal life. From age ten to eighteen, from nine o'clock in the morning to probably seven o'clock, I was in school. And school combined everything—the regular subjects with the ballet. You had a chance to learn to play the piano, learn the history of music, the history of literature, history of the theater, to learn French, learn classical ballet, the formal dance, the historical dance, partnering, acting, makeup . . . It was very comprehensive.

Who were your role models for dancing when you were young?

At that time we didn't have access to things that were happening in America, or in Paris or in London. We simply didn't have the chance to see anything that happened here. But the ballet was sometimes televised, and any person that I saw on TV, from Bolshoi or the Kirov, was an inspiration. You would see stars like Vasiliev. It was about being like those people: *I want to dance, I want to wear those tights, I want to wear this jacket, I want to look like him.*

Is it true that before perestroika you secretly watched bootlegged ballet videos?

Yeah! I think my coach was afraid,

Maxim Beloserkovsky 7

constantly being told that you can't watch Baryshnikov or Makarova because they left the country. He would bring ten boys from our class, put them in his living room, close the curtain, and put a tape on that had just a terrible quality because it was probably a third or fourth copy. But you still could see the magic, see the images, with his comments. "Look how they do this movement." I would come home and say, "My God, I just watched Baryshnikov."

Were you typecast in Russia?

When you join the theater in Russia, you start receiving roles by your look. People would say, "You—dramatic and bravura. You—lyric and dramatic." And of course by the look, I started right away with the Petipa ballets, and I did *Giselle*, and I did *Sleeping Beauty*, and I did *Swan Lake* and *Nutcracker*. And I would never do *Don Q*. I never could shift to those more bravura roles.

Were the rehearsals schedules at ABT difficult to adjust to?

It was enormously difficult. I remember the first day at ABT, I received the schedule, and I had five, six hours of rehearsal, and I was just overwhelmed. I thought it was the schedule for the whole season! But I also thought, *Oh my God, They're using me! They need me!* And then I tried to give one-hundred-percent to each rehearsal. In Russia I used to have only one coach. You have your godfather or godmother. And here you are changing studios, it's always a new person, and you don't belong to anybody. So you have to make a lot of decisions yourself. Everything happens so quickly here, so fast. There is no time, because we don't have a home theater. You don't have time for stage rehearsals. You go nuts. So it took me a while to adjust.

What are your favorite roles currently, and why?

I love all the heroic roles that I've done—because you cannot be a pirate, or the barber, or the prince in real life. It's a miracle to transform yourself through the centuries—one day you are in the twenty-first century, and the next day you move into a violent story of the nineteenth or eighteenth cen-

Maxim Beloserkovsky 9

tury, or you're a prince in the sixteenth century and you have a palace. This is the luckiest job in America!

How does the audience reaction affect your performance?

Well, to perform in New York is a blast, because, you know, people are not afraid of their emotions. They express themselves. I always felt that when you go onstage with a ballerina, or when you go onstage yourself, you have this *other* person, which is the audience. You need to bring them into you, into your dance. And you feel welcome. You feel at home. And there is nothing like that. You don't feel like a guest; you feel at home.

Do you think dancers are paid enough?

Certainly not, and I think it's so unfair. I know the ballet world is a very exclusive world. And I know that, of course, we cannot bring as many people in as baseball or soccer. But I think in the craziness of today's world, that people would come for an hour-and-a-half and just forget about their problems and transform themselves in this mystery, in these fairy tales, and cry, laugh, enjoy, and experience the emotions. I think it's worth it. Ballet dancers are paid way, way under the standard that it should be. And that's unfortunate.

What do you like most about your profession?

The constant discovery of who you are, the transformation of your personality . . . It gives you courage for your normal life. And to be so many heroes at the same time, it's fantastic!

What do you like least?

The pain. The *pain*. Unfortunately, the word "pain" is a sister to the word "ballet." There is nothing that comes without pain. It's not only physical; it's emotional pain.

Maxim Beloserkovsky 11

If you could have dinner with anyone in the dance world, alive or dead, who would it be?

Could I bring two? I would definitely love to have a conversation with Nijinsky. Maybe Sergei Diaghilev, because he was a person of unbelievable knowledge. And maybe for dessert, Anna Pavlova.

If you were stranded on a desert island, what ballet would you take with you?

Giselle. I think when I do *Giselle*, it's a feeling that I am living life in fast-forward. In an hour-and-a-half, I experience love, death, betrayal, forgiveness . . . just *everything*. Everything that could possibly exist in a human life I experience in this hour-and-a-half.

ANGEL CORELLA

AMERICAN BALLET THEATRE

Not since the defection of Soviet ballet stars in the 1960s and 1970s has a dancer created such a buzz as Angel Corella. Rumors were flying about the young talent who possessed the raw energy of a racehorse and who could toss off twenty pirouettes at the drop of the hat. After seeing him dance at the Concours International de Danse de Paris in 1994, where he won the gold medal, Natalia Makarova described him as "an angel who has been sent to us."

And never had a career been so anticipated as when Corella arrived on the New York dance scene the following year. Since then, Corella has matured from a preternaturally gifted youth to an artist who has fulfilled his potential as a bona fide star with American Ballet Theatre. And while he still makes jaws drop with his astounding jumps of compound difficulty and his cyclone-like turns, he has transformed and tempered his talent and now also rivets audiences with the depth and breadth of his stage portrayals.

The sole son of a Madrid working-class family, Corella began studying ballet at age seven with Colemar Viejo (along with two older sisters—one of whom, Carmen, is now a soloist with ABT). Although he was teased relentlessly by classmates in a country where boys are expected to play soccer and ballet is hardly considered macho, Corella persisted because dancing felt absolutely *natural* to him.

Corella continued his studies with Victor Ullate and Karemia Moreno, but felt frustrated by the lack of attention from the ballet company affiliated with the school. Determined to go elsewhere, Corella found an agent, Ricardo Cue, who entered him in the Councours International de Danse de Paris. Corella's fortune changed dramatically after that—ABT director Kevin McKenzie signed him to a soloist contract in April 1995.

Corella created a sensation in his first season at the ABT Metropolitan Opera, dancing the peasant pas de deux in *Giselle* and the Bronze Idol in *La Bayadère*. During the same season he was cast in the treacherous male lead in *Theme and Variations*, which he performed with unusual virtuosity and aplomb. In August 1996, Corella was promoted to principal dancer, gleefully adding full-length roles to his repertoire.

Since then, Corella has taken on a dizzying array of roles emblematic of ABT's eclectic repertoire. He breathes new life into classical ballets, where he often brings a sharpened focus to the male roles. After Corella's performance in *La Bayadère*, Jack Anderson of the *New York Times* wrote, "The evening was dominated by the Solor of Angel Corella. This impetuous warrior rushed headlong into the ballet's dramatic complications. Mr. Corella grew ever more exultant in the Kingdom of the Shades scene."

Corella has also made his mark as Albrecht in *Giselle*, Basil in *Don Quixote*, Siegfried in *Swan Lake*, Petruchio in *The Taming of the Shrew*, James in *La Sylphide*, and the Blue Boy in *Les Patineurs*, as well as the conflicted protagonists in *Billy the Kid* and *Prodigal Son*. Jennifer Dunning praised his Shakespearean passion when she wrote, "Mr. Corella's Romeo was an eloquent balance of naturalness and heightened ballet emotions, rushing through his short life in quick-skimming, beautifully phrased turns." A favorite of contemporary choreographers for his combination of bravura and stylistic adaptability, Corella has created roles in ballets like *Baroque Game*, *Known by Heart*, and *The Brahms-Haydn Variations*.

Corella performed at the 1996 Kennedy Center Honors and has

appeared on *Sesame Street*, dancing a tango with the letter *R*. He has performed as a guest artist with both the Royal Ballet and La Scala.

More than anything else, Corella brings a joyous temperament to his art form that is positively infectious. With flair and energy, he has helped usher ballet into the twenty-first century.

What made you want to be a dancer?

Pretty much I always knew that I wanted to be a dancer. My mother tells me that when I was two years old, I used to dance like John Travolta, because *Saturday Night Fever* was very in at that time. She said that I was out of control! I was always dancing everywhere—dance has always been part of me, and a part of the way I express myself. Music is incredibly important in my life. I always have music in my head—all the time! Sometimes it drives me crazy, but [laughs] it's beautiful!

I understand that when you were young, starting to take dance lessons, some kids teased you and even threw rocks at you.

Yeah, well that's pretty normal in the ballet world, especially in Spain. I lived in a small town outside Madrid, so I wasn't even in the city, so it was double the difficulty. I didn't have much of a normal childhood, but I loved dancing so much that I didn't miss it. When I was a little bit older, like fourteen or fifteen, I *did* want to have more friends, and all my sisters were going out with their friends and hanging around. I was always in ballet class after school and I wanted to go outside. There were a couple of times when I thought about quitting, but I just couldn't. Also, in the ballet school they were making it difficult for me as well, so it was a little bit of everything. I almost threw in the towel. I said, "I don't want to do this anymore." A month later I was back in class.

When you were young, were there any dancers that you saw as role models?

It's funny, but in Spain we didn't have access to many ballet dancers, so pretty much all I saw was flamenco. I saw a few movies where Misha was featured, and I loved it, but there wasn't a role model that made me say, "I want to be like him." I mean, I loved Misha dancing. I saw a few tapes of

Vasiliev, as well. My mother loves music and she loves dance—she's a big fan of the opera and the ballet—and she was always playing music at home. Sometimes she would buy videotapes, and I would watch them. When you are young, you just want to see something exciting, you don't want to see something like *Onegin*. You want to see some male dancers jumping around.

When you first came to New York, what were your impressions of the city, and how difficult was it for you not being able to speak English?

I didn't speak a word of English. It was pretty difficult because in Spain the family is very important—being close, and sitting down for dinner. We're a really big family and we were always together. It was really shocking, coming from a small town outside of Madrid to New York by yourself without speaking a word of English. It was a little bit overwhelming. This was my first big company! But at the beginning of my first Metropolitan Opera season, I started learning pas de deux, and learning variations, and learning everything that I was going to dance. It just became very easy—once I stepped onstage, that was it!

When you won first prize at the Concours de Paris, how did that change your life?

Whoa! It changed it upside-down! Right before the competition I was going to quit dancing, and I decided to go to the competition as a last resort. I said, "Well, I'm in this small company in Spain, and if the director's not putting me in to dance it's probably because I'm *not* that good, so I'm going to go to this competition to see what is out there, to really know my level. And if I'm not good enough, then I'm going to just quit dancing and do something else." In class I could turn and I could jump and I could do all these crazy things. I had a lot of fun doing class, and then I would go onstage and I would be standing all the way in the back. So I went to the competition and I didn't really realize what was going on until the end when I won the Grand Prix. Finally I got to that moment, to dance onstage, and that was just a thrill!

What are the positives and negatives of competing in ballet competitions?

The positive side is that it really helped me to get out of a hole, to get the opportunity to be seen. But there are dancers who have everything—they've been supported by their teachers and by their schools and they're very well prepared and *maybe*, for some reason, they don't win the competition, and they get depressed and think that they're never going to

Angel Correla with American Ballet Theatre's Paloma Herrera

make it. Also, we're talking about art, and it's hard to judge art, it's a matter of taste. But it definitely helped me.

You are obviously an audience favorite. Does the audience's reaction affect you?

Oh yeah, it does, definitely! I mean, ultimately, we're dancing for them. I can put music on in the studio and just go crazy and dance, but when you go onstage, you're really performing for those four thousand people that are watching you. It's wonderful when you feel that the audience is there with you, and they are enjoying what you are doing, so it makes me enjoy it *twice*. I think that the role of a dancer is to entertain and to make people dream, and if we do that, then that's a wonderful thing. Dance is a lot about energy, and there's a *visual feeling* you get from the audience. They don't necessarily care if your form is the "perfect form," but they're getting that energy from you, they're getting that *feeling* from you.

What made you want to dance with ABT?

All the great dancers have been part of ABT, and for me to be part of that history, it's a great honor. I hope that in the future, people will remember me as a dancer of American Ballet Theatre. It also has a great repertory, and you have the opportunity to do not just the big full-lengths, but you also work with different choreographers. It's always a process of experimenting and doing new things. I mean, they don't always *work*—they're not always a big success, but it's also good to take the challenge and to fail sometimes. Sometimes you win, sometimes you lose. Like the lottery.

What are some of your favorite roles in the company and why?

Probably because of my personality and the way I am, and the way I approach life, roles like Romeo—I love doing Romeo—because the Latin blood comes alive, and somehow, I just feel really connected to the story. *Don Q*—because I am Spanish. I love doing *Corsaire* for the blast of energy and just for being able to be completely crazy onstage. I also love roles as the Prince, which people don't always see me in because of the "ideal Prince"—a really tall, blond, blue-eyed man with beautiful feet and legs. But I've learned how to become a Prince, and sometimes I even enjoy it more than doing something that is more suitable for my physique. Just learning how to walk differently, and how to jump differently, turn *slower*—it's a totally different approach. You become a totally different persona, and the reward at the end of the show is so fulfilling.

How do you prepare for a performance?

Sometimes, depending on the role that I'm doing, I listen to certain music to kind of put me in the mood for the show. But the magic is already there when you walk onstage, so you don't really have to do much extra preparation. Once you walk onstage and you see the sets, and everybody's in costume and focused and ready to do their best, then it just comes naturally.

Have there been any performances that you felt were particularly special?

There have been some performances that are very, very special. I think the first time that I danced at the Met was a very special performance. There was a *Don Q* in my first year as a principal that I remember. I would say that every single show is a special show—a very cheesy thing to say, but it's actually true!

What do you think your greatest strengths as a dancer are?

I think I'm a very positive dancer.

How about weaknesses?

I'm still improving. I don't think any dancers are "perfect." I think you're *always* making yourself better in every aspect. There are a lot of things that I've been working on, and am still working on, but that comes with the profession. Like being a writer or anything else.

What do you like most about the profession of being a dancer?

Performing.

What do you like the least about it?

The barre. In a way, it's a strange thing. Sometimes dancers say that we're sadomasochists because we *hate* the barre, but we *love* the barre at the same time. It's a really strange thing, it's like we *hate* going in the morning—you just wake up, and you have all this nausea just from having breakfast and going into class. And that pain, all of your muscles are aching, and your calves hurt, and your joints hurt, and ahhh . . . you start a barre and then *slowly* you feel your whole body getting back together. It's a wonderful feeling.

Do you think dancers are paid enough?

No! [laughs] Never, compared to a movie star, or to a basketball player or to any other professional at the top of their career . . . *really* underpaid. I shouldn't say that, but it's true. Dancers are underpaid, especially the corps de ballet.

Is there anything that you would like people to know about you that they don't know?

I think that people really know who I am. I try to be really honest onstage, and I think people really know me. I mean, who I am onstage is really who I am. Being honest onstage is the key for a performer. You have to show *who* you are and then hope for the best. If you are true to yourself, that's the way to go.

When you're not dancing, what do you do in your off time?

I have very few hours that I'm not dancing, but I really like to go to the movies—I'm a big movie freak—and I go to Broadway shows a lot. I go to the museum. I like to roller blade. I usually go to the park—I used to go after the shows. I used to roller blade in the park at night, I found it very relaxing. I've been roller blading since I was eight years old. In my little town in Spain they have a lot of hills and I was jumping and turning with the roller blades, so I'm pretty good with them. I think when I stop dancing, I'm going to really enjoy my time. I bought a house in Barcelona on the coast—my house is hanging from a cliff. I've got open views to the ocean and that is where I'm going to come back to my senses and to my child-hood.

Would you like to direct, teach, coach, or choreograph?

I started a foundation in Spain and we're creating an international school of dance and possibly a company as well, an international company. So that's pretty much what I'm going to do with my life when I stop dancing. I hope it is not too soon, but at the same time, when I'm ready and the others are ready for me to go, then I'm going to take that step. Because I really enjoy dancing, but I wouldn't want to be suffering onstage and not be able to deliver what I'm delivering now. So at the moment that I'm feeling that it's enough I'm sure I'm going to be more than happy to walk out.

If you were stranded on a desert island with one ballet, what would it be?

I loved the pas de deux that Chris Wheeldon did for Wendy Whelan and Jock Soto called *Liturgy. I love* that music—Arvo Pärt.

Do you have any advice for young dancers aspiring to a career in ballet?

Love it or leave it! It's a really hard profession—if you don't really love it, it could be a nightmare.

Where do you think ballet needs to go in the twenty-first century?

I don't know. It's really uncertain where the *world* is going, so with ballet it's definitely even more difficult to know. I just hope that it keeps creating beauty and communicates with the audience. Hopefully it will keep going. Where it's going to go, the style, the music, the choreography—who knows? Nobody knows. I think anything that keeps our souls a little bit more motivated and positive and makes us forget about all the problems in the world, it's worth keeping it around. The arts are very important, especially right now.

IRINA DVOROVENKO

AMERICAN BALLET THEATRE

Due to the physical proficiency and unquestionable talent they display at a tender age, certain dancers are predestined to take on the mantle of *ballerina*. That was clearly the case with Irina Dvorovenko, who was the darling of the Kiev Ballet School, where she began training at the age of ten. Dvorovenko didn't disappoint any of her teachers; she has become one of the most esteemed international ballerinas of her time and a favorite with American Ballet Theatre audiences. Onstage, she is the epitome of old-world glamour and a model of the pure Vaganova technique.

At the head of her class in Kiev, Dvorovenko was always breaking barriers. When the other students were executing two pirouettes, she could do four. Her prowess propelled her into the National Opera and Ballet Theatre of Kiev, which she joined as a soloist directly after graduation in 1990. Within two years, she was awarded the title of principal dancer.

Recognized as a star in the Ukraine, she danced a variety of roles with her home company. Her formidable technique and charismatic stage presence made her a natural as the jealous princess Gamzatti in *La Bayadère* and the fiery Paquita. But, due to the flexibility of her technique and style, she was equally at ease as a delicate Sugar Plum Fairy, a radiant Princess Aurora, or a heartbreaking Giselle. The fact that she has made both Odette and Odile signature roles testifies to the broad range she has achieved in her performances.

To further prove her success as a ballerina, Dvorovenko entered numerous ballet competitions outside the Ukraine and won awards in all of them. At the Jackson International Ballet Competition in 1990 she took the silver medal, while the International Ballet Competition in Osaka, Japan, in 1991 yielded her a bronze medal. Her biggest triumph was at the International Ballet Competition in Moscow in 1992, where she received not only the gold medal, but the Anna Pavlova Prize, as well. Her last glorious win occurred when she nabbed the Grand Prix at the International Ballet Competition Serge Lifar in 1994.

Like her husband Maxim Beloserkovsky, whom she married in 1994, Dvorovenko longed to dance in the West, experience new choreographers, and challenge her artistry. Although Beloserkovsky was offered a contract with American Ballet Theatre in 1994, Dvorovenko had to wait another eighteen months until a place in the company was available to her. She was promoted to soloist in 1997, and then to principal dancer in August 2000.

As is typical of American ballet troupes, ABT put Dvorovenko to the test in a variety of roles. Some of her first assignments included the title role in *Cinderella* and the high-flying Kitri in *Don Quixote*. She brought a singular grace and virtuosity to the ballerina role in *Études*, proving her ability to shift easily from the Romantic style to the pyrotechnics of classical ballet. Her progression from a naive girl to the older-and-wiser Tatiana in Cranko's *Onegin* showed the full extent of the nuances of her artistry. And in lighter roles, Dvorovenko flaunts her enchantment and sense of humor. Anna Kisselgoff of the *New York Times* praised her "unscheduled, dazzling debut" in *The Merry Widow*, noting that "Ms. Dvorovenko is a portrait in fin de siècle presence. She knows how to carry a fan."

With her husband (and favorite partner) Maxim Beloserkovsky, Dvorovenko, now an international star, continues to move dance fans in

ABT staples like *Swan Lake, Romeo and Juliet* and the ballet she loves most, *Giselle.*

What was your training like in the Ukraine?

You know, in the former Soviet Union, there was only one way of training: Vaganova training. It is originally from the Kirov. And the system is the same in Moscow, in Kiev, in Perm, wherever in the former Soviet Union, but with a slightly different *accent*. Like in Moscow they speak Russian, but a little differently. In New York, there's Brooklyn—it's the same, English, but . . . I would say we were a little bit closer to the Bolshoi in accent.

Who were your role models when you were younger?

I didn't have the one person who was like a role model in the ballet world. It's very difficult to choose one person, because one ballerina is perfect in one role, different in another. And you may like something in one person, something in another. So you just reach out and try to find the best solution, what you would like to look like . . . You take a little from everyone.

What was your first impression of America?

The first time I left the Soviet Union I was sixteen years old. I went to America, and with the little money that I earned I bought a VCR and TV!

What was your experience with ballet competitions?

All ballet competitions, I think, are very challenging, very interesting. They kind of check you: *how strong are you?* And your personality: *how determined are you?* It is very, very important in the ballet world not to be weak. If you don't have personality, you'd better not be onstage. Because if you have no personality, you see an empty spot onstage. Very boring, nothing interesting. Very unfortunate. I like to take risks—I like to throw myself into it and try something different.

What are your favorite roles to dance?

If I am not dancing Giselle for a long time, I get desperate. I always like Giselle so much. It's a different world, a different dimension. You can express yourself in different ways, as a human being *and* as a spirit. *Swan Lake*—it's amazing in a different way. And *Don Quixote*—fabulous if you have a good mood and temperament, and you've got the fire. It depends. Every day is different, every week is different.

What usually inspires you first when you dance?

First, the music. I get a lot of inspiration from music. Music gives *feeling* to my body . . . It's a base, I think. And then the characterization you develop, the different ways you can express yourself. But if there is no good music, it's very, very hard to find something that makes you feel comfortable onstage—and a reason to *be* onstage.

How does the audience reaction affect you?

I like the warmth of the audience. They really keep us up, keep our spirits up. I can always feel the appreciation and honesty from the audience. The hardest thing is to start a performance. When the audience supports you, you feel relieved—they have accepted you and you can relax.

What is the most challenging role that you have had to dance?

Well, I would say the old Petipa repertoire is challenging. It's the hardest repertoire, because it's considered to have a perfect shape and it needs excellent training and schooling. You can't fake it. You need to keep the style, the beautiful lines, the artistry—and add some personality and sparkle to the role. If you are doing it the right way and not changing the steps, it's the most challenging repertoire.

Have you ever danced a perfect performance, or close to it?

There is, I think, no perfect performance. There is always something that could be better. You could be pleased with the performance, the audience could be, you know, turning upside-down. But still certain things could be better, could be more fluid, or your emotions could be more open.

Do you think that dancers are paid enough?

I don't think so—especially here in America. Because in the Soviet Union, the artistry was something major, and dancers were considered the way Hollywood stars are here. To be a "ballet dancer" was very exclusive. Professors and dentists didn't make as much money as the ballet dancers in Russia. "Dancing" is kind of like combining an athlete with an actor and a dancer, so it's like three-in-one, but the pay is zero, compared to everything else.

What do you like most about your profession?

That sometimes five thousand people watch you, and you bring happiness into their hearts. And they show their appreciation. I like fans very much. And I'm always very open and happy to spend some time with them—take pictures, sign autographs . . .

What do you like least about the profession?

Sometimes the crazy traveling. It's the jet lag.

Would you like to coach dancers?

I would be interested in working in a company as a main coach. I think I have enough knowledge and good taste to work with dancers and make them grow. Here in America there are a lot of good, young, promising dancers, but they get thrown into a very difficult world, and they get tested—are they going to survive or not? And many of them do not survive because a young talent is very fragile, like a flower. You need to water them and develop them, open their personalities. A lot of good dancers, I think, get injured, or ruined. You need to come into the company and be very prepared. In a Russian company they nourish you, like a mother, or like a baby, make you grow, step by step, mistake by mistake. Here, if you're strong enough, if you're smart enough, you'll work with your brain, spend some time alone in the studio, spend some time in the library, educate yourself, and learn about the ballet, about the style. It depends how serious you really are. Some people have not read *Romeo and Juliet*—and yet they are performing *Romeo and Juliet*.

ALBERT EVANS

NEW YORK CITY BALLET

There are times when a dancer relishes the stage with such complete joy that the audience becomes thoroughly infused with a similar euphoria. Such is the experience of watching Albert Evans, one of New York City Ballet's most distinct and beloved performers. Luxuriating in a movement quality that is elegant, feline, and even quirky when need be, Evans has become one of the most prominent African-American dancers in the ballet world.

Evans was lucky enough to have had the opportunity to take ballet classes at his grammar school—perhaps in itself the best argument for arts education in American public schools. As his precocious skills in dance became evident, Evans was encouraged to study ballet with Patricia Bromley at Terpsichore Expressions, a reputable ballet school in Atlanta. When his technique strengthened, he won a full scholarship to the School of American Ballet (SAB) in 1986. During the New York City Ballet's spring

1988 season, Evans was chosen by choreographer William Forsythe to create a lead role in his new ballet, *Behind the China Dogs*, for the American Music Festival. That same season, Eliot Feld spotted Evans and choreographed a solo role for him in his ballet *The Unanswered Question*. In 1991 he was promoted to soloist.

Evans has become the perfect heir apparent to many of the roles created or danced by noted former New York City Ballet dancer Arthur Mitchell. He has stepped with ease into the pas de deux from *Agon*, as well as principal roles in Balanchine's *Episodes, The Four Temperaments*, and *Western Symphony*. The delicious role of Puck in *A Midsummer Night's Dream* swiftly became a signature part for Evans. But Evans is no mere imitation; he possesses his own unique artistry. In 1995, Evans was named principal dancer with the company, where he added ballets like *Stravinksy Violin Concerto, Who Cares?, Symphony in C*, and *Symphony in Three Movements* to his repertoire.

A true choreographer's dancer, Evans has been handpicked for ballets by a number of the company's guest choreographers, including Garth Fagan, Christopher d'Amboise, Ulysses Dove, Miriam Mahdaviani, Trey McIntyre, Kevin O'Day, and David Parsons. Peter Martins capitalized on Evans's musicality and slinky speed in a wide spectrum of his works, such as *Ash, Jeu de Cartes, Slominsky's Earbox, Ecstatic Orange, Fearful Symmetries*, and *Reliquary*.

Evans has also made a successful leap from dancer to choreographer with the 2002 Diamond Project premiere of his *Haiku*, a ballet for six dancers set to a dream-like score by John Cage. In her review of the ballet, Jennifer Dunning called *Haiku* "a work as mysterious and elegant as its accompaniment." She added that, "His blending of classical ballet and the physical equivalent of dissonance is accomplished. He and his cool but intensely committed dancers have created the intriguing sense of one small and secretive beauty tucked inside another."

What inspired you to become a dancer?

The first thing that inspired me to become a dancer was seeing the American Ballet Theatre's *Nutcracker* on television with Gelsey Kirkland and Mikhail Baryshnikov. At the time I was probably nine or ten. And I was

just so amazed that here were these people dancing onstage and capable of telling a story without words. And I knew it was something I wanted to do. From that day, I couldn't stop dancing. Music would come on and I would just jump off tables and dive off my bed, because I thought I was doing a leap like Misha.

Explain how William Forsythe plucked you out of school for the premiere of his ballet.

That's a really interesting story. Here I was in Stanley Williams's ballet class, and William Forsythe walked in. And he just sat in the front of the room, watching. And he said something to Stanley. In the middle of class, he pulls me over and says, "I want to work with you after your class." I had no idea what this meant. I was just a student in the school. So we worked for an hour-and-a-half on a movement from *Behind the China Dogs*. And after that he goes, "OK, you'll have rehearsals tomorrow at New York State Theater." And I just went, "You have to be joking!" He said, "I really like your movement," which at the time was untamed. You know, here you are, sixteen, seventeen, all you want to do is just dance no matter what it is—you just want to perform. So I guess he saw something in me.

People have sometimes compared you to Arthur Mitchell. How do you feel about that?

Oh, I consider it an honor! I think it's a compliment to me. I was working on *Goldberg Variations* with Jerry Robbins—a pas de deux with Wendy Whelan—and for an hour-and-a-half he could not stop calling me "Arthur." [laughs] He called me Arthur from day one. And I told him, "Well, my name is actually *Albert*." He goes, "Oh, OK . . . Arthur, can you move over here?" And from that day on, with Jerry Robbins I became Arthur. He always called me Arthur. Always. He said, "You move just like Arthur."

Do you enjoy partnering?

Partnering has always been something that I love doing. You know, there's nothing better than dancing with someone. That's what I always wanted to do.

Albert Evans 43

What are your favorite roles to dance?

One of the roles that I really, really love doing is Puck in *A Midsummer Night's Dream*. You really get to create and to bring your personality to this role. And there's nothing better than having that freedom. Also the *Stravinsky Violin Concerto*, the first pas de deux, I really love. I've never done steps that have been so well-suited for music before in my life. There's nothing better than that . . . when the music and the steps are connected as one. It's like Balanchine said: "Hearing the dance and seeing the music." It's so true about Stravinsky.

What do you enjoy most about doing Peter Martins's choreography?

That fast footwork! I tell ya, it keeps you moving! And surprise—partnering work—he taught me a lot about partnering. He's an excellent partner. I just love it, because most of his ballets are a physical challenge just to see if you're capable of getting through them . . . you're moving from beginning to end.

What's the hardest ballet that you've danced?

Symphony in Three Movements. I've never experienced any ballet like that, never ever–because of the physicality that you're giving, the amount of energy. Once the curtain goes up, the lights are bright, there you are, you come in–there's such an entrance!–and it never stops. It only builds from there. You enter the stage at a hundred percent, and you have to give more after that.

What are your greatest strengths as a dancer?

Ah, wow! How would I answer that? I would say my greatest strength is that connection I have with a partner onstage–that connection we're trying to convey to the audience. When two dancers can give something to an audience, bring them into their performance–as opposed to *presenting* it, have them become *part* of it. It becomes a pas de trois as opposed to just a pas de deux.

What about weaknesses?

Once you become a principal dancer you realize that you really have to take control of your presentation–that you have to *give.* That was the hardest thing . . . being aware of myself onstage, how everything is presented.

What do you like most about the profession of being a dancer?

The physical activity. I love it. The relationship we have as dancers. I have my family at home in Atlanta. I have a family here, and I love it. It's wonderful.

What do you like that least?

The hours! [laughs] The hours of rehearsing! Over and over. I tell you, I prefer to perform any day than to rehearse.

Albert Evans 47

Albert Evans 49

Does it bother you that there aren't more black dancers in ballet companies?

Oh yeah, especially nowadays. It's the twenty-first century. I mean, we're capable of doing any role. So it does upset me in certain ways, you know, when I look on a stage–like here at New York City Ballet, it's–well, let's be honest, at least ninety percent white. So it's difficult, in a sense, to look at the stage and see that there aren't more African-American dancers. I think we need to reach out to those communities and say, "Look, it may be a white company, but you're capable of being part of that company." It's a dream, what's wrong with that?

Do you ever have any ballet dreams?

I do, actually, as far as choreographing goes. I may wake up after a dream with a certain idea. I visualize it and I want to see if I'm capable of choreographing something like that. A lift, you know, or certain step that may come to my mind . . . in my dream. It's amazing. I wake up, and I have to try these steps, because once you wake up, they're gone. So I usually write them down as soon as I wake up. The ballet I choreographed for New York City Ballet, *Haiku*–some of it came from a dream. The girls were floating in the air, so I turned it into walking. *Peter, did you hear that? A bigger budget! I want more money, so they can float!*

When you choreographed Haiku, what inspired you to use John Cage's music?

I've always been fascinated with John Cage. I think it's about the fantasy behind the music. In *The Seven Haikus*, there's an Asian influence, there's a Russian influence, there's an American influence. And I love that "worldly" sound–especially with percussion. I'm absolutely fascinated by that. There's a drum going, and there's a whistle, and there's a chime. Why not? I think that's music, also. Some people may think it's not, but to my ear it is. I enjoy that.

If Mr. Balanchine were here, what would you ask him?

Oh, there are so many things I would ask him. *How did he create this? What inspired him? What gave him the will every day to come up with some-*

thing new? How was he inspired? I'd ask him about all the ballets that I'm part of, and ballets that I'm not part of. And there are so many ballets that have so many inside stories to them. Little secrets. It's only when you get to learn these ballets that these things come out. And I just would love to ask him, *Where did it come from? Where? When you were walking home on Columbus Avenue? Walking to the theater? How? Or did it happen once you stepped into the studio? Or when you saw a dancer? How? What made all of that happen?* Because if you look at his repertoire, it's all completely different. And I would also like to just ask him, *What do you think of your work now? About the dancers now? How do you feel about it? And what might you change or not change?*

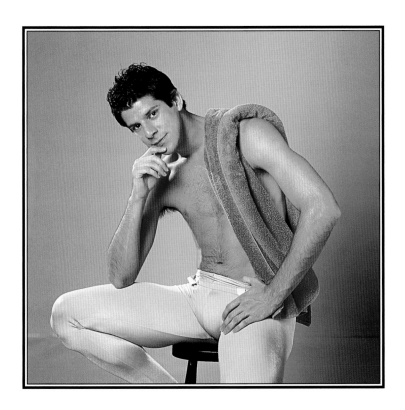

MARCELO GOMES

AMERICAN BALLET THEATRE

Brazil has always been known as an exporter of coffee, gold, and the bossa nova—but never ballet stars. Marcelo Gomes, who hails from Rio de Janeiro, may have single-handedly changed that. The most noble of princes in the classics and at the same time a hip mover in contemporary works, Gomes represents a new breed of outstanding young talent at American Ballet Theatre.

Gomes began his ballet training at age seven when a local teacher recognized his potential—specifically his musical awareness, his natural flexibility and line, and his passion for dancing. When Gomes was thirteen, he decided to study ballet in the United States. Without speaking a word of English, he enrolled at the Harid Conservatory, a high school academy for dancers in Boca Raton, Florida, on a full scholarship.

Gomes swiftly emerged as an exceptional dancer. By the age of fifteen he had developed an unusually strong technique, and his long limbs, once

gangly, were producing superb lines and a mature port de bras. At age sixteen, Gomes entered the Prix de Lausanne and took the Hope Prize, which granted a scholarship for a year's study at the Paris Opera Ballet School. After a year of grooming in Paris, Gomes accepted ABT's contract offer in 1997 and immediately began a quick ascendancy through the ranks.

Dancing in the corps de ballet, the six-foot-two-inch teenager was easily noticed and the management readily gave him challenging soloist roles. The Spanish choreographer Nacho Duato chose him for a leading part in *Without Words*, which showcased Gomes's stunning geometric lines and masculine physicality.

His versatility served him well, leading to his promotion as soloist in August 2000. As Ali the Slave in *Le Corsaire*, Gomes pulled out all his bravura technique, including multiple pirouettes and astounding jetés. He also demonstrated his understanding of the neoclassical style and speed of Balanchine's choreography in *Tchaikovsky Pas de Deux* and *Theme and Variations*. In addition, a passion for romantic roles and a finely tuned sensitivity to partnering gave him a particular poignancy as Romeo as well as Albrecht in *Giselle*.

Contemporary choreographers like Paul Taylor, Twyla Tharp, Mark Morris, James Kudelka, and Lar Lubovitch have selected him for their works because they know that his presence and intelligence in creating a character and mood, enhanced by his ability to shift gears in choreographic styles, will add immeasurably to their ballets.

Adding to its roster of astonishing men, ABT promoted the twenty-three-year-old Gomes to the position of principal dancer in the summer of 2002. As he continues to grow and thrive at ABT, Gomes has expanded his repertoire. His fiery and fun-loving Basilio in *Don Quixote* and his elegant, mercurial Oberon in Sir Frederick Ashton's *The Dream* demonstrate the malleability of his imagination and the adaptability of his technique.

Marcelo Gomes may be a Brazilian asset more valuable than gold—and more stimulating than coffee.

Do you have an artistic family?

My brother lives in Brazil and writes jokes for a TV show. And my sister works in marketing in TV. My mom writes a weekly newspaper column about fashion and restaurants. She travels a lot. She comes here and writes

Marcelo Gomes with American Ballet Theatre's Carmen Corella

about what she did—*go to restaurant so-and-so*—and she gives her rating. It's kind of like *Sex and the City* or something like that. And my dad's a lawyer.

Are male ballet dancers accepted in Brazil?

Everybody dances in Brazil. I mean, the guy that cleans the street and the doctor. Everybody goes to Carnaval and you wouldn't even believe that these people have rhythm in their blood, but they do, you know? And all of a sudden because it's classical ballet, there's a title to it. But now, thank God, there's a little bit more money for the arts, and it's starting to be recognized a little bit more. I went back to Brazil to dance, and I was received very, very well. So things do change.

What was it like coming to America?

When I came to America I didn't speak a word of English. That was the hardest thing I've ever done. I knew that if I got through that I could probably do anything.

How did the diversity of your training serve you later?

Growing up in Brazil and coming to America gave me a lot more liberty with my technique—to really show who I was onstage. In Europe they don't want that—they want pure technique. They don't want to see an individual style or personality. They want purity. Which is right for students growing up, you know. Of course, in a company you will develop a lot more of a persona; you dance more than you study. When I got to the Paris Opera School, they were like, "Whoa! You're going to calm down!" [laughs]

Was picking up different styles easy for you?

When I joined ABT I thought I was a totally classical dancer. You don't know much when you've just joined a company. I really thought that I would not be good for modern or contemporary at all. I just thought, *Well, that's OK if I'm not in that ballet, because I don't really want to try that—that's not my style.* And ABT completely got me to enjoy modern and contemporary as much if not more than classical ballet, because I just felt so free to move my body in certain ways that I didn't know before. I had so much fun! If I only had classical and I didn't have modern now, I would be hungry for something. And if I only had modern and I couldn't do *Swan Lake*, then I would be, like, *Where's my Prince?* Because I like to be romantic and I like to have all those little stories. And I also like to be real, *solid* modern: Martha Graham, Mark Morris. So I totally contradicted myself when I first joined the company.

Did you have any role models in ballet when you were training?

Julio Bocca was a very strong image for me, because he was Argentinean and grew up in Latin America. He was somebody who had made it into a big company elsewhere and had his own company in Argentina. I saw a possibility there. And now it's so weird for me to be a principal with ABT, with him being a very good friend. We share the stage together now, which is funny. But he was a big influence on me. He says to me, "Don't tell me that! I don't want to know how old I am!"

Are you a natural partner or did you have to learn that?

I started partnering when I was very young. I had a chance to work with Laura Alonso, Alicia Alonso's daughter—for a couple of summers in Brazil she came and taught a seminar for six weeks. She was definitely a tough cookie! And I was so young. I could barely lift. I was in class, and I had really tiny girls, and I had to do all the lifts. But I couldn't do it, because when you are young, your muscles are not ready for locking of the elbows, and your back is not as strong. I had a really difficult time. But it was funny, because that helped me later when I had more of an idea of what I had to do. So gradually, as I got a little older I could lift a little bit more and be more sensitive to putting the girl on her leg.

What's the most challenging role you've danced?

Albrecht in *Giselle* is pretty hard for me. My first performance, I was onstage sitting on the little bench, and I was just thinking, *I've got to get out of here!* I couldn't believe it. It was always my dream ballet. It's a very difficult role, because you can approach it in so many different ways, as if he's really in love with her or as if he's just looking for a good time. There are a lot of questions to be asked. He also undergoes a great transformation

Marcelo Gomes 61

throughout the whole ballet. And the audience can read it so many different ways. That was really difficult for me.

All the ballerinas seem to want to dance with you . . .

The girl is the first thing you see when you come onstage, not the partner. The girl is the one lifting her leg, and it's so great when you can't see the partner and it just looks like she's doing this thing by herself. And then the partner appears and it's like, "Wow! There's somebody else there!" It is

so fluent and fluid and wonderful. I really want to make the girl feel comfortable. When you have a ballerina that's happy, you don't have any problems! It makes your life a little easier!

What do you think your greatest strengths are as a dancer?

I think strength is something you get with experience. I just try to be honest when I'm onstage portraying a role. I don't try to make an extra something out of what I've already said. You don't say, "Hello, how are

you?" twice. You don't have to do an extra pirouette or lift your leg up so high to make a point. Also, a sensitivity to other dancers onstage. As much as I like to be onstage alone, I think having other people onstage really gets me going and gives me strength to do my best.

Are there any particular weaknesses that you'd like to improve?

Yeah. I think what I really want to develop is the "in-between stuff," and to make that as important as the "big steps." *How do you step onstage and present yourself just by walking?* Walking while being that certain role, or being that certain prince. How do you approach that? It's something that you can always develop. A lot of those things are visible and sometimes dancers aren't aware of them. I look at a dancer and think, *Wow, he looks like he's really in love with her.* But then he runs to the corner. And I'm like, *Oh, he's so young, He looks like he's fifteen.* It just doesn't seem like a real man. You have to learn how to do that.

What do you like most about the ballet profession?

It's being able to tell the audience how you feel through dance, without speaking. Being able to express what's inside and what I'm thinking—through movement—that's what I like to do the most. I really believe in living life to the fullest at each moment.

What do you like least about it?

It hurts a lot! It's just not natural . . . I guess pacing yourself is what I don't like about it, because you could just go *Pfft*, you know, and blow it all in one show. When I go onstage, I say a prayer that I don't fall. I believe that God hears that from me. That's very important.

If you were stranded on a desert island with just one ballet, what would it be?

Just one ballet? I'm going to say *Giselle.* Because I'm a romantic person, and no matter what you do in your outside life, that ballet will always relate to you in some way or another. It deals with dying, and it deals with . . . I lost my uncle when I was very, very young. He died of AIDS, and he was a person who was very influential to me. He took me to a lot of theater. And I believe that he would enjoy seeing me doing *Giselle,* and he would be at every performance. It is something that I would like to do a lot, so he could watch. And I'm sure he is always watching.

How do your fans react to you?

I think, no matter what, people always try to make somebody out of you onstage. They feel like they have this connection with you just by watching you onstage. I don't know how many people come up to me and say, "Oh, my God! Hi, Marcelo! How are you? I saw you onstage!" And I'm, like, "Great! What's your name?" That's the wonderful part of dance, because people just feel like they have a special connection with you.

NIKOLAJ HÜBBE

NEW YORK CITY BALLET

In a country known for great storytellers such as Isak Dinesen and Hans Christian Andersen, it is not surprising that a dancer of enormous imagination like Nikolaj Hübbe would emerge. In fact, the magic element of storytelling captured Hübbe's imagination when he first saw ballet in his native Denmark, and throughout his career he has brought wit and drama to whatever he has danced.

Hübbe follows the admirable succession of Danish male dancers who came before him, such as Henning Kronstam, Erik Bruhn, Peter Schaufuss, Peter Martins, and Ib Andersen. Like those dancers, he has combined a formidable technique in the Danish style—an articulate classical line that states rather than shouts, exquisitely balanced turns, and bounding jumps with cushioned landings—with the ability to create a presence onstage that is nothing less than honest. Whether in the Bournonville repertoire or in neoclassical ballets, Hübbe makes his roles come alive in a way that wholly inspires the audience.

It doesn't hurt that his profile could have inspired a classical bust or that his physique carries both refinement and strength. But it is Hübbe's intelligence that buoys his stage persona, whether he is delicately partnering a ballerina or careering through a virtuoso solo.

Hübbe was born in Copenhagen in 1967 and began training at the Royal Danish Ballet School from the age of ten. As a child, he danced in the children's ensemble of *Konservatoriet, Napoli*, and *La Sylphide*, a ballet in which he would eventually dance his signature role of James. At the age of sixteen, he became an apprentice to the company. That same year he was awarded a silver medal at the Paris Ballet Competition, and in 1987 he won First Prize in the Eurovision Ballet Competition. When he was eighteen, he joined the corps de ballet of the Royal Danish Ballet.

The company easily recognized that Hübbe was one of its treasures, and within two years he was elevated to the status of principal dancer. *Giselle, Onegin, Romeo and Juliet, Apollo*, and *The Nutcracker* were among the ballets entrusted to him, as well as *La Sylphide*. In 1992, after accepting an invitation from Peter Martins, he joined New York City Ballet.

Hübbe debuted with the company in Balanchine's *Donizetti Variations*, a perfect choice for a Danish dancer, with its riffs on Bournonville's swift beats set to a sunny Italian score. That summer he also tackled *Theme and Variations*. The following winter Peter Martins created two ballets on the new star: *Zakouski* and *Jazz (Six Syncopated Movements)*. New York audiences quickly embraced the new prince with the face of a handsome Viking and the heart of a poet. Hübbe shed new light on the male roles in Balanchine's

Brahms-Schoenberg Quartet, "Divertimento" from *Le Baiser de la Fee, Rubies, Square Dance, La Source, Agon, La Sonnambula,* and *Apollo.*

Hübbe quickly became one of Jerome Robbins's favorite artists, dancing *Afternoon of a Faun, Opus 19 (The Dreamer), Andantino, The Cage, In the Night, Other Dances, Fancy Free, Brandenburg,* and *The Four Seasons.* In *West Side Story Suite,* he danced the part of Riff, singing "Cool."

Hübbe's grateful partners have included a range of ballerinas, from Darci Kistler to Wendy Whelan. At New York City Ballet, Hübbe has found the perfect venue to showcase his passion and energy for the stage—he is unafraid to display his romantic side, his sexiness, his contemplative moods, and his thoroughbred contemporary style. In the ballet world he is a class act, and anyone who has seen him dance knows that.

What is your earliest memory of wanting to become a dancer?

Seeing *The Nutcracker* when I was a kid, at the Royal Theatre in Copenhagen—me and my mom and dad. It was actually not so much the *dancing* that took me, it was more the *theater*—like entering another world. Going into this very majestic hall, the curtain goes up, and then another world reveals itself. And then, funny enough, the trap doors, you know, the sets changing, the old-fashioned sort of mechanical magic of ballet or theater. I didn't think it was real because there was no talking. I couldn't get over the fact that they didn't talk. It was so weird.

Which made it more magical?

Yeah, because I thought maybe they couldn't speak. It was just so amazing! And of course the story of her dreaming, and wondering, *What's real and what's a dream?* It really tickled my fancy. It really started a big seed growing.

Danish dancers, like yourself, are trained with a keen sense of theatricality. The artistry matches the technique.

I would say so. Ballet in Denmark was very related to opera and drama. It's also under the same roof, all three art forms. And sharing the same two stages. Dance is a way to propel a libretto—there is a storyline. It was about

Nikolaj Hübbe 73

these characters, and you saw their perils—sort of like a silent movie. As a kid, that was very engaging and very educational.

Was your family supportive of your dancing?

Oh, very. In the beginning they were a bit reluctant, not of the dancing, but because of the reputation the academic school had at that time. It was called the "Dark School." They said, "What if you don't pass an exam?" Because we had exams every year to go on to the next level. They knew this was a big commitment for a little kid. But they saw that this was what I wanted, and then they said OK. They were also great because on dark winter mornings in Copenhagen, they woke me up at six-thirty to go to ballet class, and it was cold and dark, and I would go, "Oh, I think I'm sick today." And they'd say, "Really? Well, you know, you started this, you wanted this, so now you get your butt out of bed and do it!"

What did you think the first time you saw New York City Ballet?

I thought it was just like the weirdest thing I'd ever seen. It was like there was Adam and Eve, and Peter Martins was *God*. And then these women—I'd never seen women like this—they had no clothes on. It was quite startling. And also the music was so different. I remember seeing *Dances at a Gathering* and *Stravinsky Violin Concerto*.

Did you imagine that you might be dancing with New York City Ballet later on?

Not really. That came later. As I grew older, I was very fascinated by Balanchine. Getting down to the bare step—*How expressive can you make the step? How articulate can you make it? How much can the body speak just for the sake of the step and the music, that marriage?* It's so related. People tend to segregate it. You have music and a stage and people and steps, and still, the curtain goes up. People pay, whether it's a 250-year-old ballet or a ballet choreographed ten, fifteen years ago, or yesterday—it's still a theatrical art form. You can say the theatricality lies in the physical delivery, yes. But it does so, too, in *La Bayadère* or *La Sylphide*. I think, for whatever ballet you do, that's a key requirement.

What were your favorite roles when you were still dancing in Denmark?

James in *La Sylphide*. And Apollo.

What is it about the character of James that you found so appealing?

I don't know, it's very personal! It's not that he is irresponsible, but he is very much of the moment. When he is with La Sylphide, all he wants to do is run after her and go into the forest. When he is with Effie, he keeps telling her that "it's us, it's gonna be us!" And of course he is just trying to tell himself, "I love her." The first act is so restricted, and finally you let go, and it's everything you wished for. I think there's a schizophrenia there, which is interesting. He's quite mad, quite off his rocker. He has this other realm, and that's why he runs after the sylph—he follows a dream. It's like when people jump from a bridge or something!

Well, speaking of leaps of faith, how did you decide to leave Denmark and join New York City Ballet?

I had never done a lot of Balanchine in Denmark, and I really wanted to do Balanchine choreography. I was here visiting, and Peter Martins asked me if I wanted to join the company. He said to me, "If you ever get tired of being in Denmark, or if you feel you want a change of scenery, I would love to invite you to come join the New York City Ballet as a principal dancer." And I went, "All right, OK." "Now go think about it." And I went, "OK." "Do you want to come to my office tomorrow and we can talk more about it?" And I went, "All right, OK." Came to his office and said, "All right, OK. Yes. Uh-huh. Aye-aye, sir." And he said, "Well, you should think about it." I was like, "Yeah, yeah. I thought about it. It's fine." There were no qualms—I was twenty-four. I was like an electric eel in the water! Whoa!

So what was the biggest adjustment when you came to New York City Ballet?

The speed. And the massive attack of dancing so much, being onstage every night, constantly doing new ballets. And quite different ballets. One night a classical ballet, then neo-classical. One night Jerry Robbins, then Peter Martins. One night a very narrative Balanchine. And lots of choreog-

Nikolaj Hübbe 77

raphers are coming in, bombarding you. But I was just like a hungry labrador. They just eat until their stomach goes *pleech* . . .

Nikolaj, you're known for your dramatic ability. In terms of the drama, do you approach a role like Franz in Coppélia differently from Agon?

No. I don't approach them differently. With *Agon*, Stravinsky is being *super* Stravinsky, you know? And then there's Franz in *Coppélia*. It's Delibes, so . . . [sings melody]. It sounds so stupid, but you just listen to the music and do it. The steps, the music—they talk to you. I don't think you have to be a brain surgeon. It's very evident how different they are, but also very evident in the similarities. In *Agon*, you do this thing, you sort of weave upstage with the girl, and she does a huge arabesque promenade while you're kneeling. The leg goes over your head like this huge blade—images that are so startling you don't even have to react to them. It's there somehow.

So it's really about the music—

—and the steps. Like in *Coppélia*, a lot of little bounces, very dainty, like fine china. And this sweet, pink music. That already tells you a lot.

What is it that you like about black-and-white Balanchine ballets?

I like the starkness of them. It's not that they're cut-and-dry, they have such an *edge*. You know, most of them were made in the fifties, sixties, and early seventies. Even if we include, for instance, *The Four Temperaments*, which is not Stravinsky. They're evergreens. They will never fade. There's classicism in them.

What are some of your other favorite roles that you're dancing?

Sonnambula, Apollo, Duo Concertant . . . Actors are asked, "What's your favorite role?" It's the role I'm doing at the moment, and therefore that's where your soul and heart and mind are. And then there are little roles. For instance, Peter did a little pas de deux many years ago called Zakouski. And because that was the first thing he ever did for me in the company, it is very close to my heart, and I love doing it. I think maybe of all the Balanchine

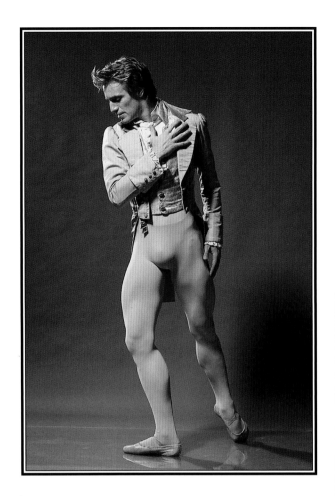

ballets, *Liebeslieder Walzer* may be my favorite ballet. Not so much to watch, but to do, to listen. It has to do with my temperament. It is very romantic. And it's so pristine, elegant, and the relationship, the care, you know, giving the hand, and touching the girl's waist, there's such an etiquette, this whole social hierarchy. You see everything there. And on top of that it is sheer *dancing*.

What did you have to learn about partnering when you came to New York City Ballet?

The idea of having the girl off-balance the whole time, and how *much* off-balance. Yeah, I would say that threw me for a loop! You know, I'm not like a Peter Martins or a Jock Soto. They just close their eyes and they can do it. I'm not that kind of partner. Somebody said that Montgomery Clift, when they acted with him, he was so much there and he was so involved with that person, whether they were having it out, or if there was a tender thing . . . I don't know if that's the truth—but I would like to think of myself like that. And that doesn't mean that I'm always physically the greatest supporter, but just that there's that kind of attention or intensity towards the girl.

What were your experiences of working with Jerry Robbins?

They were good. I liked Jerry. He always just told me to take it easy. You know, I was always overdoing everything. But Jerry loved all that—half-danced, half-marked. That was not really me, but he liked me. I don't know why. I think he liked that there was a physical intensity that sometimes got a little out of hand. And then he would scream! But he was one of those people who walked into a studio, and you grew an inch, two, five, ten . . . You knew that the moment he took over, that put it on the edge and raised the stakes. That was wonderful. And he could be so specific. When we did *West Side Story*, he was relentless. He would never stop until he got what he wanted. I remember he had a triple bypass, and he came into the theater for a rehearsal of *Opus 19*. He was out there—*with a plastic heart*—screaming over the mic. "You're not just dancers doing the steps!" That was his credo. The thing of *involvement*, that you are believable. He was in his late seventies and still harping on the same thing! And I just remember *Wow!*

*What's the most challenging role you've had to tackle at
New York City Ballet?*

Actually, it's not so much the *role* as it is the *nerves*. Maybe I can say that
I did one good *Theme and Variations* in my life, and I didn't do it very
much. And maybe *Prodigal Son*, because I did it so late. I always thought it
would be something that would really fit me, and that I would love doing
it. And I hated it! It just felt all wrong. I had expected it to be some kind of
sensation.

*Is there one particular performance that you remember as being
almost perfect?*

I probably could. But I don't want to.

Is it superstition, or what?

No. I just find it a bit . . . You're only as good as your last performance.
Even if you think, *Oh, tonight really went well,* you still have to face tomorrow. It's also a bit pretentious. Just keep it to yourself, with your mind and
soul, and then go on. I don't want to talk about all the bad performances
either! You just try to make them all good!

What do you think are your greatest strengths as a dancer?

Well, I would say the ability to step out of the wing and at least make
something happen!

How about weaknesses?

The ability to step out of the wing and make nothing happen! [laughs]

Do you think dancers get paid enough?

I think so. I mean, we don't get paid like Pavarotti. But we're different.
We're a group. Not all the dancers that you have in the group are in the
corps. There are the people who stand out and are significant, but we are,
in essence, educated in big masses.

Do you ever have ballet dreams?

Oh, yeah. Nightmares! Getting late to the theater. Whoa! Missing or not knowing the ballet. The moment you're in the wings, then you're like, *I'm in the wrong costume, and what I prepared is not what they're doing up there!* And not knowing the next step. And then there's the other dream, the great dream, the turn or the jump dream: You turn and turn and turn, and everything stops around you. And you keep turning, and you can talk to people! Or where you jump, and you jump . . . And when you land, you just go on and you jump again! And you have conversations. It's fantastic! It is the most incredible feeling of just being suspended, out of humanity, right out of nature. I guess the nightmare dream and the fantasy dream hold each other in concert.

If you were to be stranded on a desert island with one ballet, what would it be?

La Sylphide is the one that is closest to me and to my heart.

If you could have a conversation with George Balanchine, what would you ask him?

Whoa, I haven't even gone there . . . I'd just start by shaking his hand, and maybe I'll ask him if he could, you know, just "take a look and see what you think?" Or choreograph something for me . . . Or maybe I would ask him about teaching, or I would ask him about what it was like growing up in St. Petersburg as a kid. It would be a very, very long conversation! It would go on to the wee hours of the morning! Lots of vodka!

Do you have any advice for young dancers?

This is an art form that you are so lucky and so privileged to serve, and therefore you should do your utmost, and when you have done that, there's even more. Even if you just come onstage and do five steps. *What are those steps about? What is the musicality of those five steps?* You have to have a point of view and keep the integrity of it.

JULIE KENT

AMERICAN BALLET THEATRE

A blessed mixture of Botticellian beauty, gracious dancing, and the most elegant line coalesce in the form of one of ballet's most stage-worthy artists: Julie Kent. Throughout her career, Kent has assumed nearly every essential ballerina role in the ABT repertoire and has won hearts and charmed audiences in the process. Now the senior ballerina of the company, she unquestionably holds the respect of her colleagues as the reigning queen of ABT and serves as a valuable role model.

The daughter of New Zealanders who settled in the Washington, D.C., area, Kent was exposed to dance from a young age. Her mother taught ballet classes for Hortensia Fonseca, a renowned teacher, and Kent quickly became one of Fonseca's protégées. It was with her that Kent established a firm foundation and, above all, an appreciation of the aesthetics of true ballet line, one of the hallmarks of Kent's dancing. After attending the School of American Ballet and the ABT summer school sessions, Kent was made

an apprentice with ABT in 1985. In 1986, Kent entered the Prix de Lausanne International Ballet Competition, where she won a medal and subsequently became a full-fledged member of ABT.

In 1987, Kent's career took a sharp upward swing when she was asked by director Herbert Ross to star opposite Mikhail Baryshnikov in his film *Dancers*. Suddenly the limelight was cast upon the emerging ballerina, who was simultaneously being pushed into larger roles at ABT. In 1990, Kent was promoted to the role of soloist, gradually showing that she had the technique to back up her stunning looks. In roles like Caroline in *Jardin aux Lilas* and leads in *Ballet Imperial* and *Birthday Offering*, Kent demonstrated that she could carry the day. In 1993, ABT artistic director Kevin

McKenzie asked Kent to represent the company at the Erik Bruhn Prize Competition in Toronto. With her poignant renditions of pas de deux from *Giselle* and *Romeo and Juliet*, Kent took the top honor. McKenzie then promoted her to principal dancer.

Purity of style and execution lend Kent's dancing all the necessary elements for the classics. Her Odette in *Swan Lake* has joined other great interpretations of the ballet as a gold standard. *Sleeping Beauty, Giselle*, and *La Bayadère* are also works to which she has brought tremendous stature. In ABT's repertoire of Kenneth MacMillan ballets, Kent brings fluidity and femininity to a new level. Her portrayal of Juliet in the choreographed version of Shakespeare's tragic play has received unanimous praise. "Ms. Kent is an exquisite Juliet, forgoing a headstrong image for a shy young girl hopelessly in love despite the fragility she retains to the end," wrote Anna Kisselgoff of the *New York Times*.

True to the spirit of American dancing, Kent is equally at home in contemporary works. Clark Tippet, Stanton Welch, Twyla Tharp, Robert Hill, and Mark Morris have all chosen to utilize Kent's versatile talent when creating ballets for ABT. In April 2000, Kent became the only American to win the Prix Benois de la Danse in Stuttgart. Later that year she starred in the film *Center Stage* with fellow ABT dancer Ethan Stiefel. Kent is married to ABT Associate Artistic Director Victor Barbee.

For nearly twenty years, Kent has graced the ABT stage with her extraordinarily lovely presence. Hopefully, her career will last well into the future.

You're known for your beautiful line. What is the importance of that in classical ballet?

Classical line, if it's placed properly, is beautiful whether it's on Greek sculpture or a ballet dancer. It's what makes something classically beautiful. It's based on certain geometrical shapes.

How did you join ABT?

Misha called me into the dressing room onstage left at the Kennedy Center and he offered me a contract. I started crying! I was like, "I'm not ready! My port de bras is terrible!" I don't know what he was thinking, but I didn't think I was ready yet. I was in tears, and he said, "Well, if you do some training . . . What are you doing this summer?" I said, "I'm going to SAB." And he said, "Well, that's fine, you'll be OK."

How did the film Dancers *change your life?*

It was an incredible experience. It opened a lot of doors for me, and at the same time had nothing to do with my dance career. I was not really hired as a dancer, you know. Not having that pressure, I think, was a real gift. I didn't have to be anybody but exactly who I was at that moment. I didn't have to be an incredible ballerina or genius dancer; I just had to be a sixteen-year-old who was in love with Baryshnikov. And that's not exactly a stretch! There was one very dramatic scene when the filming was over. Unfortunately, all during the filming, Nora Kaye was dying of cancer, and it was very, very sad and hard for Herbert Ross, and hard for her. And so we wrapped shooting in October, and by December, Nora was really on her deathbed. We were in California on Christmas Day and were sort of called in one at a time to see her. I was called in with John Taras, and she was on her bed and was not looking very good, and she said, "So, I hear you are very good in the movie, and very beautiful. And they say you can have a career if you want it." And I said, "I want to dance." And so John turns to her and says, "And dance she will!" It was all very Hollywood!

What do you think are the positives and negatives of ballet competitions?

Well, the positives are that you see the level of your peers—especially at international ballet competitions—and you get to go see how you stand amongst people your own age. And that's an

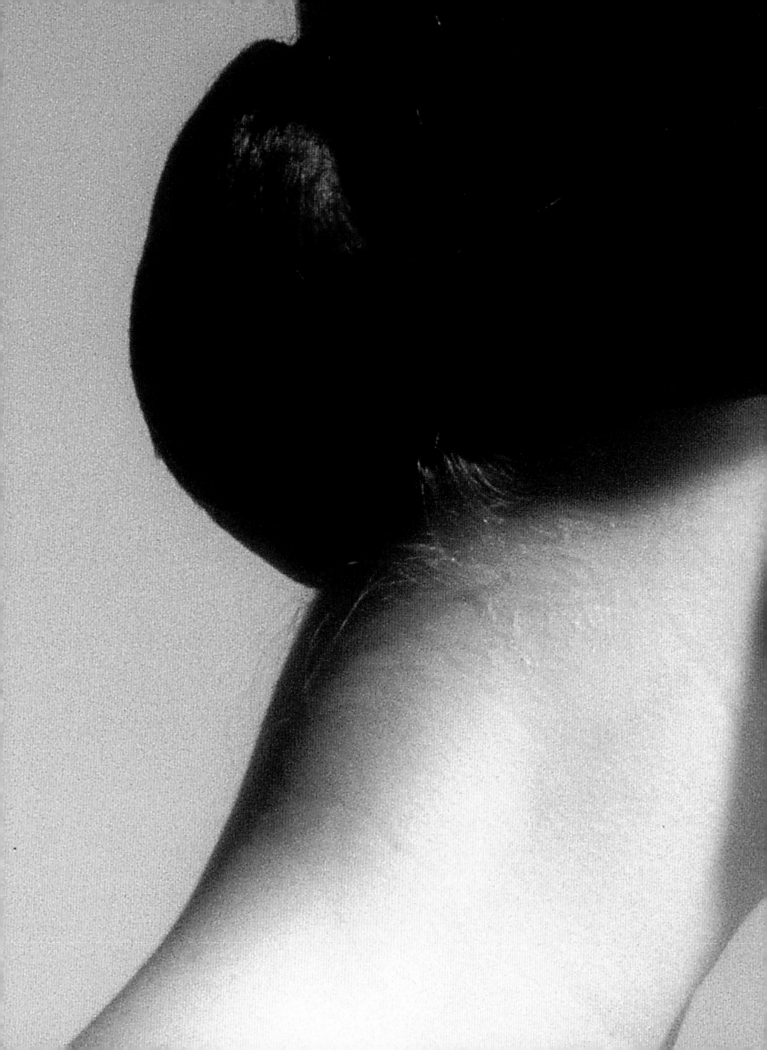

incredible learning experience. You can really judge how well you're doing, what your weaknesses are, what your strengths are, what's important to you about dancing. You start to develop your own sense of what you think is important about your work. But the only reason I did those competitions, in every circumstance, was because somebody told me to do it. It was not my idea! I think that if it's really important for you to win, then it can be a lot of pressure. I'm just not a competitive person or dancer. I mean, what am I going to do that somebody else can't do? A port de bras? I can't do more than two pirouettes, sometimes three. I don't have incredible extension; I don't have anything exceptional except myself.

What are your favorite ballets to dance?

Giselle and *Romeo and Juliet* are two of my favorites, because they're the first full-lengths that I ever did, and I feel like they're a part of me. They're just such comfortable roles for me. I know the characters so well, and dancing them is just a joy. I don't feel like there's anything that I have to overcome. I really felt a personal attachment to *Giselle*, some kind of ownership, before I even did it. It was just a *part* of me. And *Romeo and Juliet* in a similar way. As a young girl I would go to sleep listening to the music every night. I was in love with the whole ballet.

What role was the greatest challenge for you?

Don Quixote was the hardest role for me—to find a Kitri that I could really believe in. I'm just so not Latin! Not that I think you have to be in order to be an entertaining Kitri, but especially at ABT now, with so many Latin dancers—you just feel so white! But the times when I did really enjoy my performance, and felt that I did it as well as I could, were the times that I really just let go of that hang-up and had fun with it. I embraced the fact that, no, I'm not going to be the definitive Kitri.

Do you critique your past performances?

What keeps me up at night when I'm not happy after a performance is when I know that I missed a moment. I missed the timing; there was something there that I could have taken more advantage of, and I missed it. When a performance goes really well, generally my partner feels the same.

It's usually a connection between my partner and myself—that we both basically lost ourselves in the performance, that the timing was so smooth that everything just built on itself.

How do you prepare for a show?

Rehearse after class, generally. Prepare my shoes. Go home. Have lunch. Take a nap. Take Frosty out for a walk. Have to take the dog out! And then go to the theater and do my makeup and warm-up. I'm not superstitious like a lot of people. I don't have to do this and that, and wear the same tights—I figure if that's the only thing that's holding my show together, then that's pretty bad!

What do you think your greatest strengths and weaknesses as a dancer are?

It's not necessarily one thing. It's that I'm willing to completely take myself—who I am as a person—out of the equation and bring to life whatever it is that I'm dancing at that moment. There's something Baryshnikov said about when you go on the stage, you take with you every decision that you've made in your entire life. Every fiber of who you are is revealed onstage. And at the same time, it has nothing to do with me, *Julie*. It's like, *Here I am and you're watching me dance*. And some people are really willing to peel away the layers and expose their soul, personality excluded. I think that vulnerability, or that willingness to expose myself, is maybe what people find appealing. At the same time, maybe it's your greatest asset and it's also your weakest element. When you're willing to expose yourself like that, it makes you vulnerable. You don't always have the veneer that gives you power.

What makes the process of working with a choreographer unique?

I love that whole process of being a blank piece of paper and seeing how it all happens. It's just such a mysterious process, and I'm just always fascinated by it. I love to see how it all turns out.

How has your husband supported you?

My husband, Victor, has taught me to handle situations, how to

approach work, how to be professional, what's important, what's not important, how to balance it all, how to love it, how to know that it's still part of your life but it's not your *entire* life—but at the same time be in awe of the fact that we get to do it. He's been enormous.

If you were stranded on a desert island, what ballet would you want to take with you?

What comes to mind first is *Other Dances*. Because there's no story, you can do whatever you want, you know? It's like when you close your eyes and you imagine yourself dancing. Nobody's watching you. You're just in a room by yourself dancing. There's such a freedom in that, there's such a joy in pure expression. That's so beautiful and liberating. I think if I were on a desert island, there would be something really satisfying about just doing that.

How will having a baby change your career?

I'm imagining that my time in the studio, my time on the stage, and my time with my partners will be more special in that it will be my only time for myself. And every other minute that I'm not in the studio and I'm at home will be about somebody else's life and happiness, and if they're happy and fed and clean and content and sick or not sick. Every moment in the studio's going to be freedom time. And that's, as a mother, I think, a real indulgence, a really special time. I would imagine physically I'll be stronger as a person after going through pregnancy and a labor and bringing a child into this world.

What direction do you think ballet needs to take in the twenty-first century?

You hear it so much, "In my day, blah-blah-blah . . . " It's just so tired and so old. The fact of the matter is, that when people were dancing, that was the most special time in their lives. So you lose perspective on what's happening now versus what was happening when you were dancing. I hesitate to say what I think—the focus should be more on artistic performance, and less on technique. Because it's inevitable, and I think it's exciting. A lot of people that come to watch ballet don't necessarily connect with the art form on such an artistic level. If you see somebody doing some incredible physical feat, you don't have to be a sensitive person to understand that it's exciting. That element is very important, and it is going to be an essential part of captivating audiences for the next century. But it's still an art form, and the essentials of any classical art form, whether it's visual art or whatever, will always be the same—beauty, something that speaks to the soul.

MARIA KOWROSKI

NEW YORK CITY BALLET

What defines a ballerina may be an enigma, but when Maria Kowroski dances—with her bold, yet utterly feminine style, her rapier-like legs, her intuitive musicality, and her ability to take the stage hostage—no definitions are needed. When she first swirled onto the New York State Theater stage in *Serenade* in 1995, everyone took notice. With her long limbs and even longer phrases, it became evident that a ballerina was in the making.

Robert Gottlieb of the *New York Observer* stated, "Other New York City Ballet principal girls may have strong techniques or pleasing mannerisms, but since Darci Kistler twenty years ago, only Ms. Kowroski has shown us that combination of radiance and authority that identifies a true ballerina."

Kowroski bolted through the ranks in less than five years, dancing principal roles shortly after joining the company on a corps de ballet contract. As a ballerina, Kowroski has made her mark on major roles in the company's repertoire: the haunting second movement of *Symphony in C*,

the supremely challenging dual role of Odette/Odile in *Swan Lake*, and even the lovably ditsy Chopin fanatic in *The Concert*.

A native of Grand Rapids, Michigan, Kowroski began her dance training at the age of five at the local YMCA. From the ages of seven to fifteen, she studied with Charthel Arthur and Robert Estner, formerly of the Joffrey Ballet. At the age of sixteen, Kowroski entered the School of American Ballet and by 1994 had become an apprentice to the New York City Ballet and the winner of the Princess Grace award. Her first principal role, the Siren in *Prodigal Son*, perfectly suited her six-foot-plus height on pointe and her natural penchant for acting. According to Sean Lavery, the assistant to the ballet master-in-chief at New York City Ballet, "Everything with Maria is magnified so much. The steps are so clear and so large and lush."

As is the plight of many dancers, for every two jetés forward, there is one jeté back. In 1996 she sustained a serious foot injury, followed by surgery, capped by a strained back. Temporarily unable to dance, Kowroski reassessed her body alignment, read books, and spent time in Central Park. That contemplative period may have helped nudge her from being a fine technician to a first-rate artist. When she had fully recovered in 1997, New York City Ballet director Peter Martins rewarded her with a soloist contract.

Kowroski has danced luminously in ballets like *Monumentum pro Gesualdo, Vienna Waltzes, Ivesiana, Brahms-Schoenberg Quartet*, and *Liebeslieder Wälzer*. Portraying Titania in *A Midsummer Night's Dream* and leading the "Emeralds" section of *Jewels*, she possesses her own inimitable theatrical charisma. On May 8, 1999, Kowroski debuted as Odette/Odile in Martins's full-length version of *Swan Lake*. Her unending arabesque and measured phrasing helped create the effect of an enchantingly exotic bird. After her *Swan Lake* triumph, Kowroski was designated as a principal dancer.

Kowroski's latent gift for comedy—from a ballerina so seemingly serene and statuesque—surprised everyone (she can quote punch lines verbatim from Jim Carrey movies). Choreographer Susan Stroman capitalized on that looniness in the "Blossom Got Kissed" section of *Duke!*, where Kowroski played a klutzy wallflower who eventually finds a partner—as well as her rhythm. And in *Variations Serieuses*, Christopher Wheeldon's study of a backstage soap opera, Kowroski portrayed a hilariously volatile diva on the verge of a nervous breakdown, thanks to a broken ankle.

Hardly a diva, Kowroski's refreshingly unassuming attitude contributes

Maria Kowroski 103

to the human quality she brings to her roles, like her poignant performance as the Stripper in Balanchine's *Slaughter on Tenth Avenue*. With her
commanding physique and solid technical skills, nevertheless, she is equally adept at imperious or abstract roles. As the Louise Brooks—style vamp in
Balanchine's *Variations Pour une Porte et un Soupir*, Kowroski icily banishes
her sighing male suitor to a purgatory of frustration. And in *Agon*, she tack-
les the central pas de deux with the authority of a goddess.

With each season at New York City Ballet, Kowroski only gets richer in
her artistry. Chances are that dance fans haven't seen anything yet, given
that this very special dancer has not even begun to peak.

How important was your family in the pursuit of your career?

They did everything they could to get me to ballet class every day. My
grandparents, aunts and uncles . . . They were *so* supportive.

What are your favorite roles in the company and why?

The Siren in *Prodigal Son* is definitely one of my favorite roles. It's special to me since it's the first solo role I did. And also I like to do the acting
roles. I think they are a lot of fun. You don't have to go out there and stress
too much. You have to worry about props, but not the technical aspect of
it. And *Swan Lake* is just a role that I've wanted to do since I was very little.
I had seen the full-length ballet, and when I came to the company, I was
praying I was going to get it. When I finally got to do it, I was ecstatic. It
was probably the most challenging role I've ever done, but also it was very
rewarding. I felt so accomplished when I finished. It was very emotional,
too, to go from the white swan to the black swan, and back to the white
swan.

**You've sometimes been compared to Suzanne Farrell. How do you
feel about that?**

Well, initially I was very excited, because she was Balanchine's muse,
and I thought that if I have anything that she has to offer, that's great. I was
really excited to be compared to her. I know that audiences loved her. You
always want the audience to like you. I thought that if I can excite the audience the way she did, that's great; if they want to compare me to her, go

right ahead. But then the more articles that came out about it—I didn't get upset—but I just don't want to be compared to her the rest of my career. I want to be known as *me*.

Have you danced performances that you recall as being exceptional?

I think A *Midsummer Night's Dream*, that's one of my favorite parts, as Titania. It makes me feel very happy. I love the story, I love the set, I love the whole ballet and the dancing . . . I've come offstage from that, thinking, *Wow, that was a lot of fun, and I think I did the best I could.*

Are there roles that are less natural for you?

I find *Symphony in C* and *Agon* and ballets that don't have any story line a little scary. I feel very exposed. I think that when I get into an acting role, I *know* that it's not really me, that I'm playing something else. I mean, it *is* me, but it's easier for me to be told, or have a direction of what I should do. And I've actually been trying with ballets like *Symphony in C* or *Agon* to develop a little story in my head so I can put more of myself into it and make myself feel more comfortable in them.

What was your experience working with Jerome Robbins?

It was very brief. I worked with him on the Green Girl in *Dances at a Gathering* and also on *Brandenberg*. People warned me about him, saying he's very mean, and I kind of just went in there and was myself and I think he liked that, when you just showed yourself and looked like you were really enjoying what you were doing. Then he didn't really have a problem, he guided you in the right direction.

What inspires you first when you take on a role? Is it the music, the steps, or the characterization?

It depends on the role. If I've seen it for a number of years and always wanted to do it, just by watching it, that can inspire me. But I guess the music definitely plays a huge part of it, if it's something like *Serenade* or *Chaconne* or *Symphony in C*, where the music is so beautiful. The music for *Symphony in C*—I almost started crying when I first went onstage to it. I couldn't believe I was doing it. You hear the score and watch it for years, and then I went out there and in my head said, "I can't believe I'm doing this *right now*."

What do you think is the most common misconception about you as a dancer?

That I can only do adagio work. Don't get me wrong—I love to do it. I probably feel most comfortable doing it, but I feel typecast in that category. I love to jump, and I don't really jump that much. And, you know, every once in a while I'll get something like *Concerto Barocco*, and I just don't have the confidence to do it, because it happens so rarely that I get to do

Maria Kowroski 111

something out of the ordinary. I should be doing adagio roles, but I guess I feel like I need a little more of a challenge to do something harder—so I know that I can do it and not lose that confidence.

Are there some roles that you would like to do that you haven't danced?

Walpurgisnacht Ballet. That's something that would be great. Or *Allegro Brillante* or *Tchaikovsky Pas de Deux,* which I know Peter Martins doesn't see me in at all. But I would love to do something like that—even if I look awful in it, just to try it!

Do you have specific physical problems to deal with?

I'm blessed with a very flexible back. At the same time it's also a curse. My back is very long, one part of my back is tight, then it's flexible, then it goes tight again, then it goes flexible. It's hard to balance out everything. I think for the rest of my career I'll struggle with some kind of back pain.

What do you like to do in your spare time?

I love to be outside and be in nature; I guess that comes from being from Michigan. I like to read and go to the museums. The movies I like are comedies, because I like to go and laugh and not be reminded of anything that was troubling me during the day.

Do you ever have ballet dreams?

Yes. I've had quite a few ballet dreams. In some dreams I'm counting the ballet out in my head and can't seem to get it. Or I'm late for a performance and they're holding the curtain for me and I can't get my shoes on, because they won't go on my feet. Or I can't get my hair up. There's always something where I'm rushed. Something is pushing me back and I can't get there.

If you were stranded on a desert island with only one ballet, what would it be?

Well, I'm just going to say the first one that came to me: *Mozartiana.* I did it once, and it's a part that only the ballerinas have done. I always

dreamed of doing it, but it came kind of soon to me, I think. It took me to another place, that ballet. It has a lot in it. Before I had done the ballet, Karin von Aroldingen came up to me and said, "I know Mr. B. is watching over you right now. I know he is here right now." For some reason, I went out there and I did it and I felt him there. It was really great. If I were to be stranded somewhere I would like to have that feeling.

If Mr. Balanchine were alive today, what would you ask him?

If I was doing his ballets justice! [laughs] I would want to know if the ballets were being done well, and he would probably say, "You're doing them the way you think they should be done, and that's the way I would have wanted you to do them." From what I understand, he always wanted you to put yourself into the part, and not do it like anyone who had done it before.

Has your career surprised you?

I am very fortunate that I have done all the parts I have done. I am kind of amazed that it has happened so fast. Sometimes I step back and have to say, Wow, this actually happened, something you wanted your whole life. It's amazing to do all these Balanchine ballets. The musicality, the way he choreographed them—when you do them, it just feels *right.*

VLADIMIR MALAKHOV

AMERICAN BALLET THEATRE

Vladimir Malakhov is in a class by himself. He is eccentric, mysterious, and even androgynous at times, but no one could argue that his dancing is not fascinating. His particularly feline grace, combined with pristine classicism, would be difficult to find in any other male dancer.

Malakhov was born and raised in Krivoy Rog, Ukraine, where he began dance studies at the age of four at the local ballet academy. At the age of ten, his teachers urged him to audition for the Bolshoi Academy in Moscow. So, with his mother, he traveled to the Soviet capital, where due to his exceptional physique and aptitude he was accepted as a student.

At the Bolshoi, Malakhov's most demanding and impressionable teacher was Pyotr Pestov, a perfectionist who trained Malakhov to jump with ankle weights. (Jumping is Malakhov's strongest suit; he can make the audience gasp in amazement.) Artistically, the pedagogue nurtured the

young dancer with visits to museums and an introduction to poetry, and imparted to him the Perm style of ballet, which combined the *oomph* of the Bolshoi with the no-nonsense classicism of the Kirov.

For his graduation performance at the Bolshoi School in 1986, Malakhov danced a brilliant "Bluebird" pas de deux with unusually mature authority. That same year he took the Grand Prize at the junior level at the International Ballet Competition in Varna. The Bolshoi Ballet chose not to take Malakhov, but he was quickly contracted as a principal dancer by the Moscow Classical Ballet. Performing frequently, he danced many classical roles, like Prince Siefried, Romeo, and Basil in *Don Quixote*. Special roles were created for him, such as Adam in *Creation of the World*. In 1989 he won the gold medal at the senior level and the Serge Lifar Prize at the Moscow International Ballet Competition. The following year he took the bronze medal at the senior level at the Jackson International Ballet Competition.

Malakhov defected from the Soviet Union in 1990 while performing as a guest artist in California. He was invited to join the Stuttgart Ballet in 1991, but was also asked to dance with the Vienna Ballet and the National Ballet of Canada. Kevin McKenzie, the artistic director of American Ballet Theatre, invited Malakhov to join the company as a principal dancer in the spring of 1995.

Since then, he has danced a varied repertoire, including the classics, in which he is well-versed, and contemporary ballets, which he came to the West to explore. His more notable roles include *Apollo*, Solor in *La Bayadère*, Albrecht in *Giselle*, Des Grieux in *Manon*, James in *La Sylphide*, Lensky in *Onegin*, and principal parts in *Ballet Imperial*, *Études*, *Les Sylphides*, *Diversion of Angels*, and Nacho Duato's *Remanso*.

In demand as a guest artist around the globe, he has also been the subject of several films: *Bravo Malakhov, Narcise, The Dancer Malakhov, The True Prince,* and the PBS special *Born to Be Wild: The Leading Men of American Ballet Theatre.*

Did your family have a dance background?

It was always my mother's dream to be a ballerina. And she tried everything in her life. Gymnastics, rhythmic gymnastics, character dance, painting . . . But ballet has always been her dream. She said her first child would

be a dancer. That was me! So she must be very happy.

Who were your role models as dancers?

Maria Callas! I don't have role models in dancing. Only in opera. She is my idol. It's strange, but I always said, "I want to dance like Callas sings." So clean, so pure. You know, I'm not going for the *quantity*, I'm always going for the *quality*. I'm always trying to get this feeling that she had. First of all, she was a big actress. All this emotion and passion, She was never *going* for something special, because she *was* special. When you listen to the music, you always think how you can do the steps. You transform yourself . . . Well, in many of these ballets you're telling a story anyway.

Why did you leave Russia?

The idea came suddenly. I was a guest with Long Beach Ballet in California. And one night I woke up and I said, "If I go back, my life will be exactly the same. Maybe I can try to work a little bit in the West." If I went back it would have been *Giselle . . . Swan Lake . . . Sleeping Beauty . . . Giselle . . . Swan Lake . . . Sleeping Beauty . . .* But I wanted to see the world, first of all, and I wanted to work with the choreographers who would do something for me.

What are your favorite roles to dance?

Romantic roles. My favorite is Giselle. I also like Romeo. And *Bayadère*. And *Swan*

Lake. Lensky in *Onegin* was my first role when I did my première in 1989. So Lensky's an old friend!

What is the most challenging role that you've danced?

Basil in *Don Q*. I hate it so much! It's not me. Of course, all the princes and the romantic roles are easy for me. They feel like . . . *swimming*. In Vienna, the director said to me at the beginning of the season, "I will have two *Don Q*'s in May." I was suffering the whole year! I was thinking, *My God. Don Q! Don Q!* And now people remember me, not in *Giselle* or *Swan Lake,* but in *Don Q!* Weird!

What do you like most about the profession of dancing?

For me, it's my life, the dance. I cannot imagine myself without ballet. I ask myself all the time—*Every day I go in to do this exercise, and I am never bored. How can this be?* Normally people would be throwing up. You're tired. And after the performance, the next day, you go [snaps fingers] and suddenly you're fresh again, like a daisy. I never get tired of dance.

Would you like to coach or choreograph?

First of all, I am a dancer. And second, I think, I am a coach, because I have good eye. And then I can say I am a choreographer.

If you were stranded on a desert island, what ballet would you take with you?

Giselle, I'm sure. Sometimes people ask me, "If you were going to an island, what three things would you take with you?" And I always say Coca-Cola, cigarettes, and a computer or books or something . . . *Giselle* I'd have on CD.

What books do you like to read?

I like books about animals. I like nature. *What's this plant's name? And what is this bird? And where does she live? And what does she eat?* I like to be alone when I go on holiday. I try to find some place unusual. I walk for hours and hours and hours. My manager gets very worried, angry with me, because I sometimes disappear for three-and-a-half, four hours! I always find snakes or spiders . . . I once saved this pelican and carried him to a veterinarian. I grabbed his nose! My manager said, "It will be the end of your career!"

Vladimir, what would you tell a young person starting a ballet career?

Don't even start! [laughs] Some people say, "Oh, that looks so easy!" I say, "Yeah, right. It looks so easy!'" Some people come up to me and say, "Oh, you don't even use any energy onstage," or they say, "Yeah, he doesn't even have any muscles," you know? Like, some people have to fight for this, but for me it's so easy? They don't know how much I work. They don't know how hard it is, making everything look easy onstage. You must try a hundred times in the studio for one perfect performance.

BENJAMIN MILLEPIED

NEW YORK CITY BALLET

No one makes an onstage entrance like Benjamin Millepied. But what else would one expect from a dancer who radiates such Gallic charm and can make the choreography fizz like a bottle of Veuve-Clicquot? Whenever Millepied appears in a ballet, he amps the energy up to record wattage. His brilliant *ballon*, adaptability to multiple choreographic styles, and charismatic aura place him in a special light at New York City Ballet.

Millepied (whose name in French loosely translates as "thousand-footed") was born in Bordeaux, France, but raised in Senegal until the age of five. His mother, a former dancer who taught modern and African dance, began training him at the age of eight. When he was thirteen, Millepied entered the Conservatoire National in Lyon, France, studying with Michael Rahn. In the summer of 1992, Millepied trained at the School of American Ballet, then returned a year later to study on a full scholarship granted by the French Ministry. In 1994, he won the Prix de Lausanne in Switzerland.

As a student in New York, Millepied demonstrated both a noble authority and a contemporary, whiz-kid dance sensibility. Jerome Robbins took notice, casting him in a solo role for his ballet *2 & 3 Part Inventions*, performed at School of American Ballet's thirtieth annual workshop performance in 1994. The following year, when he was eighteen, Millepied joined New York City Ballet's corps de ballet.

With its rich choreographic repertoire, the company provided a hothouse environment for the eager young talent. He readily jumped into principal roles in ballets like *Tarantella, Stars and Stripes, Valse-Fantaisie, Symphony in C*, and the fleet-footed works of Peter Martins. Millepied brought a new level of virtuosity and excitement to the role of Oberon in *A Midsummer Night's Dream*. In 1998, Martins promoted Millepied to the rank of soloist.

When the choreographer Angelin Preljocaj featured Millepied in his ballet *La Stravaganza*, he stretched the dancer by casting him as an Amish-like visitor who undergoes a surreal transformation via a physical, sensual frenzy. Other choreographers followed suit, creating ballets with Millepied as a focal point. Among those were Christopher Wheeldon's *Carousel (A Dance)*, Melissa Barak's *If By Chance*, and Helgi Tomasson's *Prism*. In the latter, Millepied stopped the show with his bravura turn in the final movement.

During the last years of Robbins' life, he cast Millepied in many of his works, including *Dances at a Gathering, Brandenburg, Interplay, Piano Pieces, Les Noces, Fancy Free*, and *The Four Seasons*.

In 2002, Millepied created a sensation as a hyper-physical master of ceremonies in Mauro Bigonzetti's *Vespro*. In her review of the ballet, Anna Kisselgoff of the *New York Times* commented that, "Benjamin Millepied, throwing his body on a piano keyboard or whirling in his turns a la seconde (classical technique is not neglected), is totally in his element: a star performance."

Millepied has extended his boundless energy into the field of choreography and teaching. In 2002 he premiered his ballet *Triple Duet* at Sadler's Wells in London. He has also initiated a series of experimental choreography and teaching workshops in Bridgehampton, New York.

Not surprisingly, Millepied upholds his French heritage through his culinary expertise in the kitchen.

Benjamin Millepied 131

What made you want to study ballet?

I was taught mostly in modern, by my mother, until the age of twelve. But I think I was maybe ten or eleven, seeing films of Baryshnikov, like *White Nights*, and seeing more dance, when I decided I wanted to start ballet, so my mother actually hired a ballet dancer to teach in her school, and that's how I started. I was very attracted by the athleticism. My father was a track and field athlete. I used to go and watch him train. And I did a lot of track growing up. I was also trained in music at the same time, so I was sort of conflicted, because my father's whole side of the family were musicians, and my family felt that I had a lot of talent for music, but I decided to dance.

What instrument did you play?

Percussion. Actually, I was very good at it.

Why did you attend the conservatory in Lyon as opposed to the Paris Opera?

The reason why we picked Lyon was because my brother, who is a flute player, was planning on going there. I auditioned in the modern section, because I didn't feel prepared enough in ballet. That whole first year I had Cunningham classes every day, and some ballet. At the end of that year I decided I really would like to go into the ballet section, but modern dance was *always* very present and important in my training. Up until this time I had this image of ballet as being this really strict discipline—people being hit with sticks and so on—and dance for me was just such a joy, a pleasure, and something that I didn't associate with that sort of thing. And I saw the commentary on Paris Opera School on television when I was ten or eleven and that really just turned me off completely—I *really* didn't want to go there. I was adamant about it.

What made you want to dance with New York City Ballet?

The day I arrived in New York to attend SAB, we went to see the closing night of the spring season at the New York City Ballet. And it was just the most beautiful performance—*Symphony in C*. The energy level of the ballets, the choreography, the whole thing spoke to me and excited me in a way that nothing had before.

Who were your role models?

Baryshnikov was always one, and I think he stayed one, not just as a ballet dancer, but for what he's done for the art. He's someone who looks at dance with an open mind and a wide eye. Dance is about movement, and to me it's all the same, whether it's ballet or modern or so on, and he's still exploring. I think he's remarkable. He's brought ballets and choreographers to the attention of people who probably would never have gone to see those works. A fantastic person, really.

What are the positives and negatives of ballet competitions?

When I went to the Prix de Lausanne I was just a kid who felt that I had to do a competition. It turned out that it was a positive experience because it got me a scholarship to come back to SAB. The year after, it was good for my papers. It was good in many ways. It did some positive things. But I don't particularly feel good about competitions. The idea is not something that appeals to me at all.

How does the audience reaction affect you?

It's interesting–there are nights where you go out there and somehow everything clicks between the audience and the dancer, and there are nights where you feel that there's just nothing you can do and it just sort of doesn't happen. It's weird, but you really do feel that sometimes. We're not so much like American Ballet Theatre where they applaud every other step that you do. We're more about the work that we're presenting, so I don't really think about it too much. I think about the performance, what I'm out there to do, and about giving it my best.

What are some of your favorite roles and why?

There are roles that you can say are yours–*almost*. There are certain things that just fit you technically, musically, or dramatically. There are a few roles that I feel that way about, like Oberon in *A Midsummer Night's*

Dream. It's fantastic. There's acting involved, but there's that phenomenal scherzo in it, with that incredible music that Mendelssohn wrote when he was like seventeen. The musicality, the speed, the beats—it's something that fits my technique. The whole thing comes together. I just performed the Boy in Brown in Jerome Robbins's *Dances at a Gathering,* and that's a part I've been learning and working on for years. I don't want to say I'm a "Jerry" dancer, but I enjoy the sort of natural quality that you have to bring to Jerry's work. You're not just a dancer, you're a person. And I feel comfortable in those roles.

You also stand out in Peter Martins's ballets.

Something like *Hallelujah Junction* is very fast, very quick, and I try to do it as *extreme* as possible. You have to be driven—those performances take a *lot* out of you. Sometimes I just walk out and say, "Well, this was a good show—how the hell am I gonna keep it on that level next time I do it?" I like the speed and the clarity that you have to bring to Peter's ballets.

Are there any roles that you haven't danced that you'd really like to dance?

In City Ballet I have a handful that I'd like to do. And they're not necessarily just the parts where I am jumping around, you know, that maybe I'll do when I'm a little older? [laughs] I'd like to do *Liebeslieder*, which would require a quality that's not necessarily the obvious one that I have, but more like something that I would grow into. And sure, I would like to get my hands on *Prodigal Son* before I'm thirty.

What are your greatest strengths as a dancer?

I would hope that my strength is that when people come to see me dance, they feel that I've given a true, real performance. That's what I try to do. I respond to the moment. I hope that's what comes across the most— and my response to the music and to the person I'm dancing with.

How about weaknesses?

Partnering is not necessarily the most natural thing for me, but I'm having a lot of fun with it now. The company has such great partners. Ultimately I think I've been sort of a slow bloomer.

Do you think dancers are paid enough?

It's tough if you start comparing it to things that are really popular, like sports. Obviously, we're not in the same league whatsoever. I wish dance were more popular, that dancers could be paid more. But I think we're being paid what we can be paid. I think New York City Ballet is paid well. The orchestra has a stronger union, so they're paid better than we are. But we get a very decent salary in an expensive city. I wish there were more and more and more audiences for ballet so we could be paid more!

What do you like most about the profession of dancing?

Doing barre every day! [laughs] It helps if you have a good teacher. Stanley Williams's class was the ultimate class to take, one of the most pleasurable experiences. It really brought you into your body in a way that

classes normally don't do. Classes can be very superficial and technical, on a level that's just not *dance*. But his class was something else. And doing–taking–his barre was this sort of intense experience, and you lent your whole mind and body and physicality to it. I love rehearsing. I *love* rehearsing in studios. We have a *great* set of ballerinas at City Ballet that I really enjoy working with.

What do you like least about the profession?

Sometimes I wish people were more curious and open-minded about things that aren't really involved in their everyday job, in the arts in general. I find that dancers aren't interested in art that often. And that's one of my main frustrations. I think it's important to have a rich life experience. I mean, ballet dancers *can* tend to just be ballet dancers. And I think that's a shame. I had a great education in Lyon with my family—I was very fortunate. I think the world of ballet is just too closed up. That's my frustration.

Leading up to the war in Iraq, there was a lot of "French bashing." Did that bother you?

No. I'm as French as can be, I mean, I'm from Bordeaux, my parents are French and so on, but I've lived here for almost ten years. I don't make racial differences or "country" differences. I wasn't particularly offended. What is going on with the war, sure—*that* affects me. I mean, it bothers me that people are stupid enough to not go to French restaurants. That is ridiculous!

Is there anything you'd like people to know about you that they don't know?

Dance is *it* for me. This is my passion, my life, what I care most about. I plan to do things for it. I have ideas about how schools should be run, about how companies should be run, about ballets I want to make. For me this is not going to end in ten years. I've already started putting ideas into motion for the future. I'm starting a sort of large project—I've been given the chance to start something from scratch, with my ideas and my vision, out in the Hamptons. At this point we're starting our first artists-in-residence program, and within a couple of years it should grow to be a fairly large summer choreography institute.

I really believe in the classical idiom and ballet, but some of my frustrations are in the way things are—you either go see modern dance downtown or ballet uptown. Those things don't live next to each other in the way that they could. Now that I'm choreographing quite a bit, I've found my inspiration through the experiences in my life. The life, the things you've seen, the art you've enjoyed, all those things are what really bring you to the moment of creating something beautiful. Jerry Robbins, when he went to see a painting, he would sit in front of it for an *hour*. Very curious and educated. And the education in dance is terrible. If you are a ballet dancer, you are being taught ballet and that's it. That's a major mistake from the dancing point of view. But also, you're not taught anything about the history of your *own* art. Most dancers in City Ballet now don't know who Diaghilev was. A lot of them don't really know about Balanchine. There is a responsibility to educate dancers at *least* in their art form. So what I want to do with these workshops is to give choreographers a chance to be exposed to certain things that they wouldn't necessarily be exposed to otherwise. If we have dancers that aren't educated—where is the future of ballet?

So what advice do you have for young dancers interested in a ballet career?

Be as curious as possible. Try to see as much as you can. You know, you don't necessarily like wine the first time you drink it. [laughs] You can go to the Guggenheim and see a show and not know a damn thing about it the first time you go, but be curious and let it in little by little. Monitor what you feel. And try to develop that so you can say, "I know why I think this is good, and I know why I think this isn't good." A strong opinion is so important .

If Mr. Balanchine were here today, what would you ask him?

I would *watch* him. I would observe him—every move that he makes. I would ask him, "Take a look at my ballets and give me some advice." I would ask him for his opinion and say, [takes a big breath] "Ya know, whatta ya think?"

GILLIAN MURPHY

AMERICAN BALLET THEATRE

Gillian Murphy is a fine example of the classic success story of a young dancer, primed to be a ballerina, climbing through the ranks of American Ballet Theatre. Leggy and blonde, with a technique as accurate and dependable as a metronome, Murphy is quintessentially American in her approach to ballet; she can easily move from the classical works to the Balanchine repertoire to other contemporary works with ease. Promoted to principal dancer with the company in 2002, Murphy has rightfully been cast in a wide variety of roles, and audiences often seek out her name on the roster when securing tickets.

Although born in Wimbledon, England, Murphy and her family settled in Florence, South Carolina, when she was a toddler. It was there that she began studying ballet, becoming proficient in pointe work by the age of ten. At age thirteen, she was commuting to Columbia, South Carolina, to study with William Starrett, the director of the Columbia City Ballet. During her

tenure with the local troupe, Starrett coached her in the company's productions, including many of the classics.

At age fourteen, Murphy decided that attending North Carolina School of the Arts would provide the right balance of high school academics and dance studies on a professional level. Her primary coach and teacher was Melissa Hayden, the former powerhouse ballerina on whom George Balanchine created many of the great roles at New York City Ballet. With a steadfast emphasis on *performing* as part of the process of training, Hayden cast Murphy in lead roles in the school's productions of Balanchine ballets such as *Western Symphony, Concerto Barocco*, and *Theme and Variations*. At age fifteen, Murphy became a finalist at the International Ballet Competition in Jackson, Missippi; at sixteen, she won a Prix d'Espoir at the Prix de Lausanne in Switzerland.

When Georgina Parkinson, a ballet mistress for American Ballet Theatre, saw Murphy in North Carolina, she suggested that she audition for the company in New York. When she did so, artistic director Kevin McKenzie asked her to join the corps de ballet in April for the Metropolitan Opera season, but Murphy held off until August to complete her graduation.

Upon entering American Ballet Theatre in 1996, it was clear that her course was one of quick ascension. In one of her first solo roles, as an Odalisque in *Le Corsaire*, she knocked off an astounding diagonal of sequential triple pirouettes that opened plenty of eyes. Shortly thereafter, Murphy's debut as Gamzatti in *La Bayadère* sealed the deal. Jennifer Dunning in the *New York Times* called it "a debut of extraordinary confidence and astonishment." The attention given to Murphy's technical prowess sometimes obscured the fact that she was a major artist in the making. Of the same performance, Dunning wrote: "Technical embellishments merge with the whole. Imaginative interpretive details spring subtly from the alert physicality of her dancing. Ms. Murphy's Gamzatti, the Raga's daughter who lures Solor away and causes Nikiya's death, was one of the most touching and one of the most terrifying in recent memory. Icy, imperious disdain was evident at every moment in her poised body. Yet Gamzatti's desire for Solor was also poignantly present in every slight tilt of her head." Murphy was made a soloist in 1999 and—three years later—a principal.

Now that she is a reputable ballerina, Murphy has been fielding a wide array of roles. Myrthe in *Giselle*, Lise in *La Fille mal Gardee*, and Odette/Odile are all in her repertoire, as well as ballets by Paul Taylor, Martha Graham, and Stanton Welch. Murphy's finesse in Balanchine ballets like *Symphony in C* and *Tchaikovsky Pas de Deux* has almost single-handedly placed her as the standard bearer for that repertoire at ABT.

Exemplary of the type of career that is uniquely American, Murphy has become one of the most exciting ballerinas flourishing on the stage today.

How were you introduced to ballet?

My mother danced growing up. So when I was about three-years-old, she put me in ballet class just as an activity, you know, for no purpose of grooming me as a dancer, just something to do. And I was always running around and stretching.

I understand you danced the "Black Swan" pas de deux when you were eleven?

That was so mind-boggling! I have to show you a tape; it's really hilarious. What happened is, there's an arts festival in Florence every spring, and the Florence Ballet Company asked me, "You think you could do a pas de deux? What would you like to do? You could do whatever you want." And I said, "I'd like to do 'Black Swan' pas de deux!" [laughs] And I could only do, I don't know, like sixteen fouettés at that point. Still, at age eleven, a lot of girls are not even prepared to do anything *en pointe*. For some reason I felt always comfortable in pointe shoes. But it's crazy looking back at it, because I was so tiny. I was sort of a late bloomer, and I would go in the studio every day and make myself do an extra *fouetté*. I got up to thirty-two, and did the performance with this guy who had danced with Alvin Ailey. He was twice as tall as me. It was really funny. But I loved it.

Gillian Murphy 149

What was it like coming to New York to live and work?

I guess I was very focused on dancing and learning. And I don't mind being by myself; so that was a good thing, because at first I didn't know anybody. There was an adjustment period, definitely. And also I missed nature. All these people running around. It's a little overwhelming—but you get used to it.

Now that you're at ABT, what are your favorite roles and why?

Some of my favorite roles are Hagar in *Pillar of Fire* and Odette/Odile in *Swan Lake*. The beauty of the choreography and the musical scores are endlessly inspiring, but the most fulfilling aspect of these roles is the transformation that the characters undergo.

When you're preparing for a role, what do you think inspires you first, or inspires you most ? The music, the choreography, or the characterization?

The music plays a large part, because you can get carried away with the character and where they're coming from. But when you break it down, you listen to the music and sometimes it's not that complicated. It's always intriguing to go from just doing steps to thinking how much there has to be a motivation behind each movement.

How do you prepare yourself? What's the process you go through?

Well, I guess there are the rehearsals, and then—I love to read. Sometimes if I start reading a book, I don't want to do anything else!

What kind of books do you like to read?

Books like Herman Hesse's *Siddhartha*, where characters really create a path for themselves. Or else, like, Gabriel Garcia Marquez, that type of literature. I also enjoy reading poetry—works by Walt Whitman, for example—and any literature that takes you into a different realm, that's inspirational or just makes you think.

Did you ever take any motorcycle trips with Ethan Stiefel ?

Yeah! On the back. It's fun. I like traveling, open air . . .

**What do you think is the most challenging role you've undertaken
so far?**

Definitely Odette/Odile. Especially the White Swan. Because of the vulnerability and the delicacy of the character. You know, once I get in the studio, I'm ready to move—like big moves—but the real test is to bring the subtlety of movement and emotion to the surface. So that requires a little more from me.

Would you like to dance Giselle?

It took me a while to picture myself as Giselle. But it's something I'd love to do eventually. It's an amazing role. Every ballerina should do it.

What do you think your greatest strengths are as a dancer?

Gosh, I don't know. Well, I think turning or jumping. I don't really have to think about those things, so I have the freedom to use my imagination and to hopefully create something more than just steps.

You also have a very natural line.

I wouldn't have said that! I always feel like that's something I need to work on. I guess I could use better extension. I'm trying to create something a little bit more magical than just acrobatics.

Do you think dancers are paid enough?

Well, I don't know what's going to happen with the future of ballet, but I think somehow we need to get people excited about it. We can't expect to get paid that much more when there isn't a real sense about the greatness of ballet in our culture. It's a shame we don't get paid more because the artistic value and dedication of ballet dancers should be worth millions of dollars.

What do you like most about being a dancer?

The performance is a huge thing. I just thoroughly enjoy it. Also the process—but when I was younger, that's not what I would have said. You realize how much you can learn if you're constantly thinking about a role in the rehearsal studio—thinking about it and developing something. I would hope to transport the audience. That's the goal.

What do you like least about being a dancer?

There are a lot of egos. Growing up I encountered some characters. What I don't like is that you can see someone give a mind-boggling performance, and so few people might get it. People's taste sometimes really boggles me. The people who have real integrity in the art form aren't always the favorites.

Do you ever have dreams about ballet?

In our performance season I do. I've had "turning" dreams before. Yeah! I just keep on going. It's pretty fun. I think before I danced *Tchaikovsky Pas de Deux*—because I only had a few days to prepare for it—I was having these dreams where it was just the steps sort of going in a loop.

Is there anything else that you would like to add?

My progression from being in the corps has been gradual and not overwhelming. That's really important, because the timing seemed right. I've gradually gone from Odile to Gamzatti to *Études*, so I feel comfortable now. When people get thrown on as child prodigies, it could create a sort of fear to change. I just feel fortunate that I am in a company that I love. And I'm inspired by the other dancers daily, I like how they each have a unique approach.

JENIFER RINGER

NEW YORK CITY BALLET

Only a few ballerinas, like Jenifer Ringer, are blessed with that particular gift of dancing that seems to engage the audience in a conversation. Each detail and nuance of her dancing seems to spring from an inner source, with a warm generosity that soars clear up to the fourth ring of the New York State Theater. Her patently lyrical brand of dancing manifests itself in a port de bras that speaks eloquently, a movement quality that sings outward, and a manner that communicates lovingly to her partners.

A Southern-born beauty—quite capable of physically passing as the ballet world's version of Scarlett O'Hara— Ringer also possesses the tenacity associated with the heroine of *Gone with the Wind*. Rare are the dancers who quit their careers due to burnout—and are still able to recoup lost time when they decide to make a comeback. Yet Ringer not only survived—she prevailed. After leaving New York City Ballet as a soloist in despair, she returned triumphantly, soon to be promoted to the rank of principal dancer.

Born in New Bern, North Carolina, but raised in South Carolina, Ringer competed with her older sister, who excelled in music and sports. She started dancing at the age of ten in Summerville, South Carolina, and immediately clicked with ballet's physical and musical challenges. At age twelve, she began studying at the Washington School of Ballet, where she encountered Balanchine's style for the first time in *Serenade*. After a year of training on scholarship with the School of American Ballet, she whizzed through her apprenticeship and became a full-fledged corps de ballet dancer with the New York City Ballet in 1990.

Ringer caught the eye of Jerome Robbins, who knew her fresh all-American approach, combined with an appealing femininity, would work in his ballets like *Interplay*, *The Concert*, and *2 & 3 Part Inventions*. After charming audiences in 1992's Diamond Project, Ringer was selected by Peter Martins, Miriam Mahdaviani, and other choreographers to create roles in new ballets. As she continued to work her way into the repertory, Ringer felt herself start to slide. She gained weight, sustained a back injury, and suffered from depression. Although the company promoted her to soloist in 1995, she wasn't managing the stress levels. By 1997, she agreed mutually with the New York City Ballet management that she needed time off; the decision to return was left to her.

The period that followed evolved into a time of introspection for Ringer. She stopped dancing altogether and completed her degree in English at Fordham University. Slowly and somewhat reluctantly, she made her way back to ballet class at her own pace; gradually, she felt confident in returning to New York City Ballet, dancing select soloist roles in *Divertimento #15*, *In the Night*, and *The Four Seasons*.

A turning point arrived in 1999 when Twyla Tharp chose Ringer for a ballerina role in *The Beethoven Seventh*. Her appointment as principal dancer in May 2000 paved the way for Ringer to widen her artistic scope.

Ringer has found a particular niche in New York City Ballet in ballets that showcase her lush, romantic movement quality, like *Brahms-Schoenberg Quartet*, *Dances at a Gathering*, and "The Man I Love" duet from *Who Cares?* Proving herself capable of carrying an entire evening, Ringer is a radiant and inexhaustible Aurora in *The Sleeping Beauty* and a capricious Swanilda with a crackerjack technique in *Coppélia*.

In July 2002, Ringer and James Fayette, also a principal dancer with the company, married, and their partnership onstage reflects their bond off-stage. Ringer continues to shine in ballets by Balanchine, Robbins, and Wheeldon, among others. For this ballerina, setbacks never precluded a comeback.

What was your first big leap into the world of ballet?

I remember the audition for the Washington School of Ballet was so intimidating I cried in the car for thirty minutes and I didn't want to go in. All the girls had matching uniforms on, and it was just frightening. Especially coming from a small ballet school in South Carolina. It was a big eye-opener to me just to be in a class of very talented girls.

Is there a ballet that is particularly special to you?

Serenade has, funny enough, been kind of a theme in my life, because my very first experience with it was at Washington Ballet. The experience of performing *Serenade* at the Kennedy Center was really what made me want to be a professional dancer. That was like a lightning rod! *Serenade* was also my first performance in the New York State Theater. And then later, after being away from the company for a year, and then coming back, I danced the Waltz Girl. It's been a really important ballet for me.

What made you want to dance with New York City Ballet?

I always thought that I would want to dance with ABT, and I really hadn't heard that much about New York City Ballet, because they didn't tour that much. But once I had seen the company perform and I had seen the ballets they do—the Robbins, the Balanchine—just the way the dancers moved, it seemed so free, and exciting, and . . . *windswept*. And I just thought that that's what I want to do. I wanted to move like that and dance those ballets.

What was your experience of working with Jerry Robbins?

I loved working with him. It will always be one of the honors of my life. It was such a privilege to work with him. And we actually had a great relationship. I've always loved his ballets. I love the fact that they tend to be *real* people dancing. *Dances at a Gathering* is such a special ballet; you feel like part of a family, and you're onstage for an *hour*. You know, you're not necessarily a ballerina in his ballets, you're a real person expressing yourself by dancing. And he always stressed the relationship between the dancers and the eye contact between the dancers. That's always been something that I've found the most satisfying about performing. Really, everything about his ballets just felt right to me.

In your first years with the New York City Ballet, how did you negotiate the low points?

I got into the company when I was sixteen, which maybe for me, was too young. It was a dream come true, and I was just so thrilled, but I had never even thought about the negative aspects of a job. I just thought that dancing professionally would just be heaven every day! I don't think I was prepared for how tired I would be, how much I would hurt sometimes, and how sometimes performing wouldn't be fun, because I was so exhausted. I would use food as a stress reliever or an emotional crutch, and I gained a lot of weight. I remember getting promoted to soloist and assuming that it would solve all my problems and that I would be happy—and then realizing that being promoted really didn't bring me happiness. I ended up depressed. I hated my dancing. And it came to the point where it was decided that basically I needed to get away from the company.

What got you back on track?

When I finally went back to class, I was a good forty pounds overweight, but that was the turning point. I actually managed to look in the mirror and like myself the way I looked at that moment. I took baby steps from then on.

Since you acquired your college degree, how important do you think continuing education is for dancers?

It's huge. A lot of people don't realize what a big deal it is. It definitely helped my dancing, just to read some Henry James and Edith Wharton and to take a painting class—to do things that were completely different from

ballet but definitely have a bearing on ballet. It made me feel more well-rounded as a person. But also it just gave me more confidence. A lot of dancers are so crippled by fear of just normal dealings with people in the outside world.

What have been some of your favorite roles?

There's *Serenade*, of course. *In the Night* is very special to me. It really is just a great ballet. And you know, any time I can dance with my husband is wonderful, like dancing with him in *Brahms-Schoenberg Quartet*, the second movement. That was one of my first big roles. I love the lush, romantic, lyrical kind of dramatic ballets. I just love the dancey things.

What's the secret behind your endless stamina? You don't seem to sweat.

I sweat! I always feel like I'm the sweatiest person out there! I always trust in the fact that I'm going to have a little bit extra, and hope that I do. I *believe* that I'm going to have the energy. But, you know—this is probably something that none of the other dancers will say—but a lot of times to prepare for the season I take cycling classes at the gym. I'm addicted to them! When I rehearse a ballet, a week before the performance, I try and run it as much as I can . . . just to see what it's going to feel like.

What are your strengths and weaknesses as a dancer?

I think that maybe I'm good at carrying a feeling throughout a ballet, or characterizing something. I think maybe from the waist up I'm better than from the waist down! I've always felt more confident with my port de bras and my interpretation of a ballet than with my technique.

What is your experience of dancing with your husband?

James and I love dancing together. Because we had the professional relationship before the romantic relationship, we are still able to be professional in the studio and still work well together. Being husband and wife has just been kind of a nice addition to that.

Is it true that you like science fiction novels? How do you reconcile **Brahms-Schoenberg Quartet** *with H.G. Welles?*

I've always loved the science fiction–fantasy genre. I have a big imagination, and they stimulate that. I love to completely escape and go to a different world. I don't like to read things about real life. I like to read about things that are going on in Middle Earth—Hobbits and stuff like that!

What would you ask Mr. Balanchine if he were here now?

I'd ask him about changing that thing in *Donizetti Variations!* No . . . [laughs] His ballets are very self-explanatory. I mean, they're all so musical. I don't do some of his more complicated leotard works—what I tend to do of his rep are the more straightforward pink or blue ballets. So I don't know if I'd have any questions about specific steps or anything like that, but I think I would ask him *What is the most important thing for a dancer to think about during his ballets?* Is it the music? Is it the choreography? Is it the projection and the feeling? I know there are a million quotes out there, and a lot of them are taken out of context, and may be contradictory, but I would love for him to say, you know—"Just dance!"

Is there anything that you would like people to know about you that they don't know about you?

I'm interested in writing books for children, and I've been writing things for years . . . But I'm just now trying to get the courage to send them out to agents.

JENNIE SOMOGYI

NEW YORK CITY BALLET

Sometimes a dancer flies under the radar, continually surprising the audience with her authority, versatility, lyricism, and musicality. Such is the case with Jennie Somogyi, who has quietly taken her place among the best of New York City Ballet's ballerinas. One of the company's strongest technicians, she is a dancer's dancer whose talents extend far beyond her flair for jumping and turning. In the last few years, Somogyi has demonstrated a facile ability to take on a wide variety of roles, forging her unique style with feminine strength.

Robert Gottlieb of the *New York Observer* summed up Somogyi's stature: "The company does have a brilliant classicist in Somogyi. She's admirable in the daunting First Movement of *Symphony in C . . .* and in *Who Cares?* ("Embraceable You," "My One and Only") she's the one you can't take your eyes off, she rips into the steps with such bold joy." In another review he stated, "She's also moved triumphantly into the more romantic ballets, for which her intense musicality and her expansive movement are so suitable. In the Heather Watts role in *Davidsbündlertänze*, she gave a revelatory performance, deeply felt and thrillingly danced; the whole balance of the ballet changed."

Born in Easton, Pennsylvania, and raised in a blue-collar family in Alpha, New Jersey, Somogyi studied gymnastics as a child, then segued into ballet at the age of seven, because she adored the music. She trained with Madame Nina Youshkevitch until the age of nine, when she enrolled at the School of American Ballet. At ten, she demonstrated precocity for technical strength and a feeling for the stage, when she was cast as Marie in Balanchine's *The Nutcracker*. Within five years, Somogyi was made an apprentice with New York City Ballet and, at age sixteen, entered the corps de ballet.

With her confident, quick-study approach, Somogyi was promoted to soloist in 1998. Maneuvering from allegro to adagio roles with aplomb, Somogyi found the Balanchine repertoire an excellent fit. Her speed and power gave her an edge in *Allegro Brillante, Ballo della Regina,* and *Tchaikovsky Pas de Deux*. But her fluent lyricism also allowed her to excel in ballets like *Liebeslieder Walzer, Brahms-Schoenberg Quartet,* and *Raymonda Variations*. Her Dewdrop in *The Nutcracker* is a perfect study in rock-solid technique and full-bodied musicality.

Upon her promotion to principal dancer in 2000, Somogyi clearly proved her ballerina mettle, revealing her dramatic gifts in the Robbins repertoire and shedding new light on her roles in *The Cage, Brandenberg, Dances at a Gathering,* and *In the Night*. In Balanchine's *Episodes*, Somogyi lent an air of mystique reminiscent of Allegra Kent. Debuting in the dual role of Odette/Odile in Peter Martins's *Swan Lake* in 2003, Somogyi assumed the challenge with natural ease, making her portrayal an unqualified success.

But for all her glamour and Amazonian prowess onstage, Somogyi is hardly a diva offstage. Married to a policeman with whom she shares a home in New Jersey, she sheds her ballerina persona at the stage door of the New York State Theater and heads home to watch the Yankees game on television or spend time outdoors.

For a while, Jennie Somogyi has been New York City Ballet's best-kept secret. But when she steps into the spotlight, the praise only gets louder for this exceptional ballerina.

What was your early training like?

My teacher, Nina Youshkevitch, was great. She was very strict, but she had a soft side to her. She really pushed you, but she wasn't intimidating. I think that was the perfect mix for my age. She used to say to me, "So what if you fall? I'll pick you up." You know, "Just *try* it." In those early years she really had me try everything, so that I knew I could do it if I needed to. I think that gave me some confidence.

How did the demands of ballet affect your childhood?

I kept a very normal childhood. And even when I was in high school, I would go home, and go to football games with my friends on the week-ends, which I think was really important because I don't feel like I missed out on anything. I never went through that kind of rebellious phase that a lot of people get into, when they get older and discover that there are a lot of other things out there.

Did your family keep you grounded?

When I first got into the company, I was seventeen. I remember the first day of our layoff—I'd just finished a season working so hard. I was just so happy to sleep in. I went to bed that night, and I was like, "I don't have to do anything tomorrow." And my dad busted open my door—"C'mon, you're going to learn to change oil!" At eight o'clock in the morning, I was in his garage in my jeans learning how to change oil.

Have you always striven for versatility in your career?

I've always thought it was kind of sad that people get labeled and put in a box. I was, kind of, when I first got in the company. I could jump and I could turn, so I started to do a lot of those kinds of roles—firecracker roles. And I didn't necessarily relate to those roles. That was kind of a struggle, because I was a little concerned that I maybe was being pigeon-holed—I didn't feel like that was really what I wanted to express. You can't be in that same mood all the time! So eventually they started putting me in different things, and that was great, because they saw that I could do different things. My rep is definitely more diverse, and I actually get more compliments in the lyrical things than I do for those firecracker roles.

How did you prepare for Swan Lake?

It's funny—a lot of people say, "Do you watch videos? Do you go back and watch the originals?" And I don't actually like to do that. I just didn't want to see anything. I wanted to have a blank slate and just figure out what was coming out of *me*—and what I wanted to do with it. Because I feel like sometimes I watch other people do something, and I can almost see the wheels turning—they saw someone else doing it, and they're trying to recreate *that*. I want it just to be natural and be my interpretation of something. When I had to do *The Cage*, I had only seen Wendy Whelan do it, and I was like, "Uh-oh, I'm not gonna look like Wendy." I mean, she's amazing in it. So I just blocked it out and started over. And I came up with a very different sort of insect . . . more like a spider.

What have you learned from dancing Balanchine's choreography?

The main thing is to trust your instincts. Everything that he choreographed feels very natural; it just flows. It's almost like you don't even have to think about the steps. Everything makes perfect sense—*Well of course I would do this step next. It just fits perfectly in the music.*

How do you maintain your focus with the company?

I'm the kind of person that, if you just say "Good" to me once, it makes a world of difference to me. It'll really keep me going, and make me push harder. It's just those little encouraging words. And you know, when you're in a company, there's not really time for any one mistake.

What are your favorite roles and why?

I love *Serenade* just because it's *Serenade*! [laughs] I love the music. We just brought *Brahms-Schoenberg Quartet* back, and I usually do the first movement, which I just love, because it's—I guess *lush* would be the word. Usually my favorites are roles where I cover a lot of space. And that doesn't necessarily mean it's fast and jumpy, but, you know, just where I get to *move*. I always feel like there's something really satisfying in the ballet when you feel like you've just covered a lot of space and you've said what you wanted to say.

What do you think are your greatest strengths as a dancer?

Oy! I guess that I'm musical. A lot of times that saves me, because I just let the music tell me what to do.

How about weaknesses?

I have a very hard body where I'm very loose-jointed. And so even though I'm muscular and I'm strong, everything is so much harder for me to pull together.

Are there any performances that you remember as being particularly exceptional?

I've had a couple of shows where everything just felt really right. Last summer we were in Saratoga, and I did *Symphony in C*, first movement. And it was the last show of the last night, and we were all exhausted. I was so tired, but somehow . . . The music was the perfect tempo, and everyone knew it was the last show. Everybody was looking at each other onstage, and I remember that was like, *ah!* What a great way to finish! Everyone was connected. The audience, everyone onstage . . . It just felt *right*.

How did you hook a cop as a husband?

I have always been interested in criminal profiling, you know, for the FBI. That was kind of my big thing. [laughs] When I meet people, I don't remember the name, but I always kind of feel people out, and I'm very into how people think. So I've always kind of been interested in that field. I met him when he was going to the academy, and we became really good friends. I was always really interested in what he was doing with his job, and . . . we just hit it off. And so we dated, I guess for not very long, before we got married.

So when you stop dancing, will you work for the FBI?

I would love to, but I think my husband would probably kill me! No! [laughs]

How does your personal life affect your stage persona?

Who you are is inevitably going to come out when you're onstage. If you have no experience in your life, you're not going to have anything to dance about. Maybe that's why I can do a lot of different types of roles—because I have a lot of different sides to my personality.

What do you do with your free time?

I don't do Pilates or any of that kind of stuff! I'd rather go hiking and swimming, do stuff at home.

What do you like most about the profession of being a dancer?

I like that my job is physical. I like that you get to express whatever you're feeling. I listen to great music all day. And I like to travel.

What do you like least about it?

How many hours of your life it can consume. When we start a season, it's almost like you're putting your whole life on a shelf. There are a lot of thirteen-hour days, and you have to go home and sew your shoes for another hour or so, and so sometimes it's a little too consuming. Sometimes what we do allows no time for anything else.

What would you ask Mr. Balanchine if he were here?

When you dance his choreography so much, you feel like you kind of know him or understand him. I don't have any questions for him. We always get little stories from our ballet masters—Sally Leland is great for those. Every role you do, she tells you, "Now I remember when Mr. B. said this about . . . " But I think one of the greatest things I've ever heard that he said—or that people said about him—was that he always gave you *back to yourself*. That's how I like to picture him, just looking at who the dancer was, and that people said they weren't afraid. He would say, "Fall. That's good, it shows that you have energy." Sometimes I think, "Oh, I don't know if I'm going to do this part justice," and that's when I tell myself, as long as I go out and do it full-force . . . He probably would have said you couldn't really go wrong if you followed your instincts.

Are there any misconceptions about you?

I think a lot of times people think that I'm very tough and strong, and that's not me. My close friends always tease me that I put on a very tough front, but I'm actually very sensitive.

ETHAN STIEFEL

AMERICAN BALLET THEATRE

Ethan Stiefel relishes the fact that he is an American-bred star in the international world of ballet. In the spirit of American hybridism, Stiefel never concentrated on one style of ballet, but immersed himself in whatever dance forms he could learn. A beloved principal dancer with American Ballet Theatre, he has appeared as guest artist with the great ballet companies of the world, like the Royal Ballet and the Kirov Ballet.

Critics and fans have marveled at Stiefel's graceful coordination, musicality, energy, and impeccable line. In every sense, he has proved himself to be one of the most versatile and stunning American male dancers of his or any generation. Yet, an unassuming modesty as refreshing as his onstage bravura accompanies that singular talent. "I have rarely encountered anyone who combines as Ethan does a sense of the importance of what he does with a modesty and grace about who he is," said Nicholas Hytner, who directed Stiefel in the movie *Center Stage*. "Believe me, you don't encounter that combination very often on a movie set."

Born in Tyrone, Pennsylvania, Stiefel was raised in Madison, Wisconsin, where his older sister Erin studied ballet. So that the hyperactive eight-year-old wouldn't tear up the house, Stiefel's mother brought her son along to dance classes. Stiefel became a natural copycat for ballet and any type of movement. In junior high school, despite his involvement in track and wrestling, his parents racked up mileage taking him to ballet classes and performances in Milwaukee and Chicago. When his family

moved to Pennsylvania, he trained with Marcia Dale Weary. His father (a former Lutheran minister turned prison warden) transferred to a job in the federal prison system in New Jersey, enabling Stiefel to attend the School of American Ballet—and become serious about ballet.

In 1989, at the age of sixteen, Stiefel not only joined the corps de ballet of New York City Ballet but also won a silver medal at the Prix de Lausanne competition. Wonderfully polished in the Balanchine style, Stiefel excelled in ballets like *Divertimento #15, Symphony in C,* and *Tchaikovsky Pas de Deux,* as well as *Dances at a Gathering* and *Interplay* by Jerome Robbins. By age nineteen, Stiefel had been promoted to principal dancer with New York City Ballet and had been awarded the Princess Grace Foundation USA Emerging Artist Grant. Stiefel took a leave of absence from New York City Ballet in 1992 to join the Zurich Ballet for a year, but returned to the company a year later. In 1997 he joined ABT as a principal dancer.

Even among the splendid male dancers of ABT, Stiefel holds a special place on the company roster. In the "Junk Man" pas de deux from Twyla Tharp's *Known by Heart,* Stiefel methodically and sensually rips up the stage. His *Prodigal Son* stands out as a sensitively and athletically rendered portrait. And as Albrecht in *Giselle,* the transformation from a romantically reckless youth to a man of mature gratitude and love is authentically yielded in Stiefel's interpretation of the role.

Sir Anthony Dowell, the former Artistic Director of The Royal Ballet, specifically chose Stiefel to appear in Dowell's signature role of Oberon in the ABT premiere of Ashton's *The Dream.* "Not only is he a wonderful dancer, but also an accomplished and self-effacing partner, " said Dowell. "These latter qualities were much enjoyed by those who danced with him."

In May 2000, Stiefel thrilled moviegoers (especially teenaged girls) and rallied a new audience for dance with his film debut in *Center Stage* as the cunning, swaggering Cooper Nielson, a ballet superstar with an offstage libido to match his onstage pyrotechnics.

Whether Stiefel is dancing on the big screen or in ballets like *Fancy Free, Apollo, Les Patineurs, The Sleeping Beauty,* or *Push Comes to Shove,* all eyes are on him. He's an American original who knows how to honor the traditions of the past, the adrenaline of the present, and the expectations of the future.

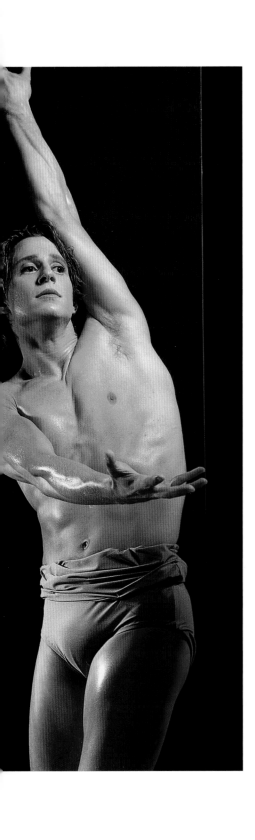

What drew you into taking ballet classes?

I'd always been pretty physical and active. Both my sister and I had been in gymnastics. I was pretty hyper. I wasn't like a Ritalin kid or anything like that, but I was into playing sports all the time—that included in the house—and I broke a lot of furniture and put holes in walls and stuff like that.

How has being an American star influenced your career?

I came from the classic Dolly Dinkle School where you have everything. But it's one of my frustrations that Americans don't seem to play on the same level as if, say, I came from the Paris Opera or the Mariinsky Theater, or Royal Academy. And that's not to take away anything from them. I feel sometimes that they don't look at *who* is in front of them and what he or she is doing. It's, "Where do they come from? What is their history?" And in that sense it's a bit frustrating, because the United States doesn't have the tradition that these other schools have. What happens is that sometimes someone coming from outside of those circles can be seen as not legitimate.

Were your parents supportive of your dancing?

My parents, man, are unbelievable. We haven't touched on the number of miles that they put into it. First, they drove forty-five minutes to Madison, then they drove two hours to Milwaukee. And then I started performing in Chicago with the Ruth Page Foundation, and that was *four* hours. They definitely sacrificed a lot, and they are a big part of why I danced. People are fascinated that my dad is a prison warden, and they think he's going to be this hard-ass dude. I guess what was most fascinating for me was that a lot of the inmates were pretty impressed that I was a dancer. It may relate to the fact that they saw that I had the freedom to do something quite liberating.

Do you think that you have paved the way as a different type of ballet dancer?

People may say "he's one of the finest American classical dancers of the past forty years," and it's nice to read that, but it's also sad, because there

were a lot of people before me who weren't recognized. They struggled. And I don't know what will be in the future . . . America has always been progressive, or at least it likes to think so. Why does ballet need to maintain this kind of "holding on" to what was? Yeah, you need to do that, but ballet needs to go *forward* as well. Music has gone forward, art, photography . . . Dance seems to be one of the things that *will* go forward, but only as fast or as far as certain people want to let it. And that's not the spirit of why we're into it.

Is ABT a good fit for you now?

Definitely. Even from day one it had a certain vibe or atmosphere, that there's work to be done—everybody knows that—but it was just a really mellow group of people. Coming from a company which has a very defined vision, and is only in one theater all the time, can have its limitations. When you're a touring company and you're doing a full-length one night and a contemporary thing the next night, it gives it a different feeling. It allows me a chance to pursue other stuff, which was important to me and is one of the reasons why it works so well. ABT is the place for me because going into the new roles, the company has been patient. I've been able to go into roles in a good way. Kevin McKenzie has put me into them personally. I've had people overlooking me and developing me in a good way. It would be different if I just had to go out there and produce. I felt like that the first season I was there, just because of my own insecurities and so on. But the atmosphere of the company keeps it grounded.

What are your favorite roles that you are dancing now?

Albrecht in *Giselle* seems to have a special place for me. The hardest part for me was to make Albrecht into someone who was not just an asshole. Many people say he is a cad. I don't believe that one hundred percent. There's got to be something a little more going on, or it doesn't read from the first act to the second act. For

Ethan Stiefel 189

me it was a matter of trying to maintain his nobility and his self-centered-ness, but at the same time having a sensitivity underneath that keeps him human from the beginning and throughout.

Did you enjoy singing in West Side Story Suite?

When I sang for Jerome Robbins in the rehearsals I had to do a little voice change. He said I sounded like Bob Dylan!

When your are preparing for a role, what is it that inspires you first? Is it the music, the steps, the characterization?

What inspires me first is the physical aspect, just because that's what I tune into. Going into a role I need to set up a foundation of what's going on physically, what's my relation with the characters, what's my relation between myself and the audience, you know, even where am I on the stage. Once I get a feeling for that, then the music and the choreography come together. When I'm preparing for a role, things come to me. Sometimes rehearsals can be the worst time for me to go forward. I may be home doing something completely different when something comes up.

Is there competition among the guys in ballet class?

Yeah, I would say so. We say, "Let's go for this," or "Let's see if we can do that." I'm not saying that I'm *not* competitive. The competition is instinc-tual. I try and make it something positive, something that is going to be productive for me. Otherwise, I would just have to quit [laughs]. You'd just sit there and say, "Jesus, look at what *that* guy is doing!"

How do you prepare for a show?

Before a show I'll play whatever song I like at the moment, something with heavy bass and a big beat. Something that gets the adrenaline mov-ing—probably to the dismay of some of my roommates in the dressing room.

Were you ever cast in a role that you initially thought, "There is no way I can do this"?

Yeah, there have been plenty of them! Like Lensky in *Onegin*, just because it's very adagio. It's not something that I am used to doing. I guess when something is really slow for me, it really sets off alarm bells.

Have you ever had a perfect performance where everything came together?

There have been performances, where when I'm done, I've said, "All right, that felt good." But there's never a perfect performance. I guess it's my Germanic heritage—it's my instinct to want perfectionism. But I want to approach it so that it doesn't matter. That has been the most liberating thing.

Do you consider yourself a workhorse?

I'm sort of like a thoroughbred—and they race once a week! Not that I only need to dance once a week, but you know what I am saying. I go out there and go balls out, man, one hundred percent.

What do you think your greatest strengths as a dancer are?

My feet! [laughs] No, I'd say my greatest strength is that I have my own perspective and that I stick with it. Not that I am not open and ready to take criticism and correction, but I have my own take. I think that my greatest strength is that I believe in what I'm doing, although it may not be to everyone's taste.

What about weaknesses?

I have to concentrate on my pas de deux work. I'm a small, lightweight guy. And so if I'm with the right person, it's not a problem, but I'm not the type of person who can just go and work with anyone.

What's the most common misconception about you?

Probably because of the actions I've taken, as far as taking control of my career, people would assume that I'm arrogant or ungrateful or something

like that. That's pretty painful to hear, because that goes back to my parents. That's the last thing I would want. I'm trying to be straightforward and honest, and sometimes in this business that isn't taken as being genuine. To be really direct can be taken as being difficult.

How did Center Stage *change your life?*

I get letters from people saying they enjoyed it or that they've never seen dancers or that they've never seen dance. And that's kind of cool. Then you get the people who you don't even know if they've seen the movie, but they like to collect autographs. I try to answer everyone. The Ansonia Post Office hasn't had to create an area for me, so it's not that crazy!

If you were stranded on a desert island with only one ballet, what would it be?

That's *heavy.* I would say the melancholic section from *The Four Temperaments.* I danced it once, by default. It's amazing music, big time.

Would you like to choreograph or direct a ballet company?

If I were to stay in it after retiring as a dancer, it would be as a director. I have spoken to directors, and I say, "Why can't you be a director that remembers how it was to be a dancer?" And to their credit, they say, "We all go into it thinking we're going to do that." But then for whatever reason, that's not the way it works. But I don't believe that. I might be too Midwest and wholesome and unjaded, but I think that there are ways to maintain respect and let people have their dignity, to be honest about stuff and do the hard things. The reality of the business says it's only for so many people. I might be a little idealistic in my approach. But you've got to go there. You can't say you only want to be *halfway* decent. I am dedicated to developing American dancers. It's time that really does happen—before it's too late.

Would you like to add anything else?

No, I'm fried.

WENDY WHELAN

NEW YORK CITY BALLET

In the history of New York City Ballet, Wendy Whelan stands out as one of the most stunningly unique and breathtaking of ballerinas. Perhaps, more than anyone in the company, she has bridged the gap from the twentieth century to the twenty-first. With her improbably streamlined body, she transforms her dancing into dynamically geometric art. Musical, versatile, intelligent, and fluid, Whelan continues to amaze dance lovers with her ceaseless evolution.

Born and raised in Louisville, Kentucky—perhaps not coincidentally famous for the thoroughbred racehorses with which Balanchine often compared his ballerinas—Whelan started dancing at the age of three. Whelan's mother, a gym teacher and basketball coach, couldn't contain her daughter's energy, so ballet classes proved to be a perfect vehicle for her natural athleticism. As a child, Whelan studied with the Louisville Ballet Academy and performed with the Louisville Ballet in *The Nutcracker*. At

thirteen, she was given a summer scholarship to the School of American Ballet; two years later she attended as a full-time scholarship student. Whelan was asked to join the corps of New York City Ballet in 1986.

Peter Martins quickly recognized that Whelan had ballerina potential and utilized her talents as a featured dancer in his *Les Petits Riens*. In 1989 she was promoted to the rank of soloist. Whelan first made her mark dancing principal roles in Balanchine's "leotard" ballets like *Stravinsky Violin Concerto, Symphony in Three Movements, Agon,* and *The Four Temperaments.* As she advanced, becoming a principal dancer in 1991, she proved her wide range, demonstrating the clarity of her classical technique and dazzling presence in the ballerina roles of *Symphony in C, Swan Lake,* and *Allegro Brillante.* Jerome Robbins also adored Whelan, capitalizing on her dramatic physicality as the Novice in *The Cage,* as well as lead roles in *Dances at a Gathering, Brandenberg, In Memory of . . . ,* and *In G Major.* More recently, Christopher Wheeldon, using Whelan as his muse, has revealed some of her unparalleled abilities in his ballets *Polyphonia* and *Liturgy.* And William Forsythe and Twyla Tharp chose Whelan to enhance their ballets, *Herman Schmerman* and *The Beethoven Seventh,* respectively.

In the last few years, Whelan has combined her strength with softness and lyricism in romantic ballets, such as *La Sonnambula* and *Brahms-Schoenberg Quartet.* When Whelan starred in the revival of Balanchine's *Ballade,* Anna Kisselgoff of the *New York Times* praised her extraordinary performance. "Like an autumn leaf, Ms. Whelan floats in a bouree, and yet beneath the fragility there is a stunningly tensile performance," wrote Kisselgoff. "She has only to dip in a swoon in the first duet, to weep in a brief solo, to throw herself toward Mr. Tewsley in an arched shape to register the passion below the surface . . . truly an affair to remember."

It would not be hyperbolic to say that Whelan's dancing often approaches the miraculous.

Was ballet easy for you as a child?

The physical aspect of it was. I was a little slow to learn the mental aspect of it, coordination, and to understand musicality. I was regularly frustrated by it, but for some reason I didn't give up—I always wanted to be in the shows. I enjoyed the learning process, working one-on-one with the teachers. And I got attention that I didn't get at home from my mom, who was overwhelmed with the kids.

What was it like attending the School of American Ballet in New York as a young student?

I moved here when I was fifteen to go to SAB. The training was a little different. Immediately I felt very strong, very capable. I think the teachers felt that in me right away, they kept advancing me levels. I wasn't afraid. I had a really strong focus on school and ballet. I wasn't on the streets playing around. I didn't have that kind of curiosity for goofing around. And that's why I think my parents thought I could do it. The day of my first SAB workshop performance was the day Balanchine died, April 30, 1983. That was my first performance onstage. I woke up that morning to get ready for the show, and I heard on the radio that Balanchine had died. My response was, "Uh . . . what's going to happen?" And bigger than that, "Where am I going to go?"

What made you want to dance with New York City Ballet?

My teacher, Robert DiCello, always thought that I had a certain kind of linear feeling that would be correct for that. And then I started to see the ballets when I was here. I would see *Agon*. And I would see that chic, very sophisticated quality, and it was like the fashion pages, but alive, and in motion with this incredible music. And I just fell in love with the aesthetic of Balanchine. I'm still overwhelmed by it and feel so lucky.

What have you learned from dancing Balanchine's ballets?

It's interesting, because I've been dancing them for almost twenty years now. And I regularly find new things in each ballet. I've learned different things about myself, as a person. I used to do a lot of leotard ballets—I still do. And that was my first love, because of the athletic quality and the abstraction. But now I'm finding myself in the more romantic ballets, and I'm drawn towards that quality. And I'm sure in the next years I'll find another realm of what he's done that reaches some other part of me, and teaches me something about who I am, and draws out something in me. I think that's very exciting, as a human being.

What was your experience of working with Jerry Robbins?

I was very tough on myself; I wanted everything to be perfect. He saw me being difficult with myself backstage, going over something. He came up to me and said, "You know, Wendy, the audience is here to enjoy you, so just let them." He saw me struggling, and I think he liked that in a person, because he had that quality in himself. He liked that I didn't wear a lot of jewelry, I didn't wear make-up. It was all about the work—it wasn't about anything other than *process*. Because I really love process, more than the outcome, even. When I was ready to dance *The Cage*, he let me go with it. He didn't come back with notes or corrections. He sometimes would fix my wig. But I felt like he was patting me, and saying, without words, "You're doing just fine." I could make him laugh, at the end, when he was tired. I think he wanted me around him, because I added to his energy level. All I had to do was look at him and he would start laughing. We connected. I miss him a lot.

What keeps you motivated as a dancer?

If you can't do the classical things, well, you're not really on top of your game. If I'm not nervous about something, then the edge gets lost, I get bored. I don't have that next lily pad to jump to get across the pond.

What are the most challenging roles for you?

The romantic ballets like *Sonnambula* were not natural for me. As dancers mature and they mellow out and maybe find some kind of love in their life, then that's interesting to play around with onstage. You hear the music differently when you actually know what that feels like inside you.

You have the reputation of being a workhorse at City Ballet.

It's interesting, because I look back and I see a couple of years in my life when I really felt like I was holding the company together, because a lot of principals were injured. And I also was having a hard time in my personal life. Peter Martins and Rosemary Dunleavy really valued what I had to offer them. They said, "What do you need? Do you want to go to Hawaii?" Anybody else would say, "Yes!" But I actually said, "I need to dance all the time, because that's how I'm going to get through this." And so I did *The*

Cage and *Swan Lake* in the same night—the birds and the bees all in the same program—and it was thrilling! But at the same time, I didn't really have a life and it was covering up stuff that was going on. I didn't know myself except as *the dancer*. And then this strange injury came along, because my body didn't know how to turn off. This one leg muscle didn't know how to relax. So I had to take some time off to slow down. I couldn't really jump with strength for a year. And with some acupuncture, Rolfing, massage, and a different way of thinking, I put my energy into myself as the *non*-dancer, and I worked on that, and learned to like myself for who I was when I wasn't getting applause. I got a little bit of balance back in my life. And my body balanced out, too.

What makes your working relationship with Christopher Wheeldon special?

When we did *Polyphonia* and *Liturgy*, it happened so fast—it's was like *gestalt* or something. It was Jock Soto's input, my input, Christopher's input—things just kept getting layered and layered. One idea would lead to the next, and everything just fell right into place.

What have you learned from working with different partners?

Jock is the one who taught me how to be partnered. To *become* partnered. Because I was always considered so strong technically, the guys would just think, "I don't have to turn her, she's just gonna turn!"

Are there any roles that you haven't been cast in that you'd like to do?

Sure, there are tons of them, but I really trust Peter, and I've never really gone to ask him to learn anything. Because I trust his opinion and what he thinks is right. So he'll put me in a part that I'm like, *What are you thinking?!* And maybe he's wrong sometimes, but a lot of times he's shockingly right. I am very grateful—he's given me so much to do.

The question of weight and body image has often been discussed in the context of your career.

I can tend to get thin, but I really don't think I could've had the career I've had, doing two ballets a night for a number of years, without being strong. If you're too thin or weak, you can't do that. People have a right to what they think, but–for the books–I'm a very healthy individual. I've always been a muscular person and very lean. I've seen European people come to this company, and they come in soft. And we do things so fast, and we work such long days, that they look like different people now. They look like whippets, and they came in looking like fluffy poodles.

Is there anything people don't know about you that you'd like them to know?

I'm a funny person! I think I come across so serious in ballets. But I'm a pretty silly girl. I don't know if people realize that.

What do you think your greatest strengths are as a dancer?

My athleticism. I have a curvature in my spine, and it forces my body to move in a different way that's a little off-kilter. Maybe that adds something interesting to the way I do a step, in an off-balance kind of aesthetic. It's atypical. My devotion to the work is a very strong aspect of what I do, and I think people can see that. And I hope that my gratitude for what I do comes across, because I try not to take any day in this building for granted.

How about weaknesses?

Finding a softness in my body, because it's naturally so hard. I have a strange juxtaposition of confidence and lack of confidence. I came to New York with tremendous confidence, but at the same time I've been given ballets to do where I can't stand up before I go onstage because I'm so nervous.

Were there any performances that you've danced where you thought, "That was as good as it gets?"

There have been performances that I've thought, *I'm in God's hands right now, and God is letting me really feel this.* One of them was my first *Mozartiana*, and one of them was my first *Swan Lake*, the Balanchine version. My first Dewdrop. And each of those were the performances where I could not stand up beforehand, where I had to leave class because my legs wouldn't hold me!

***What do you do now with the little
time off that you do have?***

My boyfriend is based in Los Angeles,
so I really enjoy going out there. He has a
little house in LA, a Venice bungalow. We
just hang out, see his friends, and go to
museums there. And so . . . maybe I'll be
there one day.

Do you ever have any ballet dreams?

My dreams tell me what's going on
with me. A lot of times I'm watching other
people dance. But I have a lot of dreams
about buildings, and I always feel like the
building is me. And whether the doors or
windows are open relates to a door or win-
dow or part of my body that's open.

***What do you like most about the
profession of being a dancer?***

I like the people I work with. I like the
creative process. There's just a certain
kind of different connection you make
with the people that you dance with—big
sisters, little sisters, brothers, lovers, it's
such a family—a weird, close thing. There
are connections that are indelible.

***What do you like the least about the
profession?***

The knowledge that it'll be over.

If you were stranded on a desert island, what ballet would you want?

Oh, my God! Can I pick an evening of ballets? I think *Liebeslieder Walzer* would be one. Maybe *Sonnambula* would be another one. Maybe *Jewels?*

What would you ask Mr. Balanchine if he were here?

I would thank Mr. B. first. Then I would ask him, "What is it that I still need to find in your ballets?" I think that's all.